Rachel's Favourite Food for Friends

RACHEL ALLEN

GILL & MACMILLAN

Gill & Macmillan Ltd
Hume Avenue
Park West
Dublin 12
with associated companies throughout the world
www.gillmacmillan.ie

© 2005 Rachel Allen

ISBN-13: 978 07171 3999 6

ISBN-10: 0 7171 3999 9

Photographs by Suki Stuart
Food styled by Laragh Stuart
Index compiled by Cover to Cover

Book design and typesetting by Anú Design
Colour reproduction by Typeform Repro, Dublin
Printed by GraphyCems Ltd., Spain

A catalogue record is available for this book from the British Library.

7 9 8 6

Contents

Romantic Dinner for Two

Party Food

Summer Lunch

Midweek Supper Party

Formal Dinner Party

Girls' Night In

Chocolate

Barbecue

Curry Night

Afternoon Tea

Acknowledgments

I dedicate this book to the three gorgeous boys in my life: my husband Isaac, and our sons, Joshua and Lucca.

Where would I be without my amazing family? My sister Simone, who I ring at least three times every day for chats, advice and inspiration; her husband Dodo, who puts up with me ringing three times a day; their two brand-new twin girls, Rosa and Lola, whose arrival from Vietnam we have all been so excited about; and Mum and Dad, who I also seem to ring three times a day — you have all been so incredible; thank you, darlings.

Thank you so much, Darina and Timmy, for the huge support and for allowing me to use lots of recipes from the cookery school, not to mention the constant supply of herbs, eggs and vegetables from the farm.

A huge thanks to Antony and Jay Worrall Thompson who are always so kind, and generous with their advice. Thank you too to my lovely agents, Fiona Lindsay, Leslie Turnbull and Linda Shanks, at Limelight Management.

A big thank you to Fawn Allen and Bree Watkin, who helped me with the typing when I got completely snowed under. To all my other friends who helped me in so many other ways, with inspiration, support and cups of tea.

And last but not least, thank you to all at Gill & Macmillan — Michael Gill, Nicky Howard, Aoileann O'Donnell and Emer Ryan — for making this book what it is. A very very special thanks to Suki and Laragh Stuart for being so stylish, as always. Speaking of style, thank you, Beth Haughton, for always being there with your vision! A very big thank you to David Hare, Producer and Director of *Rachel's Favourite Food* and *Rachel's Favourite Food for Friends*, and also to Billy Keady, cameraman; Ray de Brún, sound; Neil McLaughlan and Kevin Lavelle, editors; Anna Ní Mhaonaigh, production assistant; Sally Walker, production manager; and Sarka Pizlova, kitchen assistant.

Rachel's Tips

Sugar

At home, I now use only unrefined sugar, which comes from the sugar cane, because I believe that it is better for you than refined beet sugars, and I prefer the flavour, too. Trace elements of various minerals are found in unrefined sugar, and as a rule, the darker the sugar, the more 'healthy' it is. Unrefined sugar is now available in most shops and supermarkets — for example, golden caster, and golden granulated sugar, golden icing sugar, light muscovado and dark muscovado sugar; just look for 100% unrefined cane sugar on the packet.

Olive Oil

I tend to have two types of olive oil in my kitchen, both of them always extra virgin, which is much healthier than the inferior-tasting 'pure olive oil'. For cooking, I normally use a decent basic extra virgin olive oil; and for salad dressings, or drizzling raw onto vegetables or bread, I use a really special olive oil. Olive oils vary, so it is worth tasting a few (dip a bit of crusty bread in) to see what you like. Store your olive oil away from direct sunlight.

Spices

For the best possible flavour from your spices, buy them whole, and crush or grind them when you need them; the difference is amazing when they are freshly crushed, as opposed to buying ready ground. But if you are crushing spices and have some left over, just store them in an airtight jar, and use within a few weeks for best flavour. There are some spices that are available only ready ground, and they are: ginger, cayenne pepper, chilli powder and turmeric. I use a mortar and pestle to crush a small amount of spices, and an electric spice grinder, or coffee grinder, to crush a larger amount.

If you fry spices in a dry pan for about 20 seconds until slightly darker and toasted, they take on a totally different flavour — almost nutty. This works very well for cumin and coriander, and the added beauty is that it makes them easier to crush by hand. If you don't have a mortar and pestle (and I find that the ceramic ones are not so good — the spices go flying everywhere), you can put the spices into a plastic bag and bash them very well with a rolling pin or a weight.

Chocolate — How to Melt, and What Type to Buy

Good-quality dark chocolate should have at least 50% cocoa solids, but try to use chocolate that contains between 60 and 70% cocoa solids; chocolate that contains much more cocoa solids than that gets quite bitter, which is great for some recipes, but not all. Decent milk chocolate for cooking with should contain at least 30% cocoa solids. Some chocolate 'purists' claim that white chocolate is not real chocolate at all, but technically it is, as it does contain cocoa butter, even if it doesn't contain any cocoa solids. Look for a really good white chocolate for the best creamy, mildly vanilla-ey flavour. Above all, avoid what is often labelled as 'cooking chocolate'.

Chocolate must be melted gently. I normally place it in a heat-proof bowl (not metal) over a saucepan of barely simmering water. In fact, you can place the bowl on the saucepan, and once the water underneath has come back up to the boil, just take it all off the heat and it will continue to melt as it sits over the steaming pot. Chocolate melted in a microwave, on a low setting, also works well, or chocolate melted in a very low oven.

Store your chocolate somewhere cool and dark, and away from the children!

Citrus Fruits

If limes, lemons, oranges, or other citrus fruits are not labelled as un-waxed, scrub them with warm water before grating the zest from them. Use a very fine grater (I love the American micro-plane graters, or something similar), and just grate the top layer of zest; if you grate till the peel is white, you have gone too far, and it will be very bitter.

Salt

I keep two types of salt in my kitchen. One type is plain dairy salt (it is usually sold in a bag in supermarkets), preferably with no anti-caking agents. I use this for cooking, as such — putting into water for pasta, or into a sauce while it is cooking, or into a bread or a cake, as it is so fine in texture. The other type is sea salt — my favourite is the English Maldon Sea Salt. It is in small flakes that you can crumble with your fingers, and I use this for seasoning things — salads, vegetables, meat or fish — just before serving them. I love the little bursts of flavour that you get when eating it. This is the salt that I would put on the table, too.

Pepper

I find the flavour of black pepper ground straight from a pepper mill much better than ready ground. For sprinkling on certain salads, meats or even vegetables, sometimes I prefer to have the pepper slightly coarse, so I crush a little using a pestle and mortar.

Vanilla Extract

The flavour of vanilla extract is a lot better and purer than the sometimes quite synthetic vanilla essences that are available. Vanilla extract contains (by law) at least 35% alcohol, and is not sweet, but 1 tsp of it will transform a simple cake or ice cream. I buy Organic Madagascar Bourbon Vanilla Extract, which comes in a 118 ml (4 fl oz) bottle, from my local health-food shop. When compared ml for ml with the smaller, cheaper, not so good essences, it is not that much more costly.

Seasons

Eating according to the season we are in is not only much more healthy for us, but much more enjoyable too, not to mention all the air-miles that seem to be struck up bringing French beans, for example, all the way over from Africa, and eating them in December, after they have been sitting in a warehouse for two weeks before finally reaching our table. Why not enjoy them in July, or whenever they are in season for you, when they will actually taste of something, and be far more nutritious besides? And if we really think about it, that's what we and our bodies actually need. Nature has it right giving us blackberries in September, packed with vitamin C, to prepare us to fight those autumn colds. Moreover, it makes cooking, and eating, a bit more interesting, having a dinner party with the first of the asparagus of the season, or wild salmon, or autumn raspberries, or what-ever it is you look forward to!

Order of Work

Anyone reading this who has ever done a 12-week course at the cookery school will laugh, as we always go on about the order of work, but I think past students will also say how invaluable a list, or order of work is, when you are entertaining for a large group of people, or have many elements in your menu to think about ... or maybe I am just a bit keen on my lists, or forgetful even!

A very basic order of work may look like this:

Previous Day	–	Make ice cream and freeze
5.00pm	–	Make soup
5.30pm	–	Make pasta sauce and set aside
6.00pm	–	Wash lettuce for salad and make salad dressing and set aside

Christmas Dinner

At some stage or another, most of us get the job of cooking Christmas Dinner, which is no mean feat. This is a meal for which you will definitely need to be very well organised because, as we all know, there are so many other things to do on the day — not to mention trying to get dressed in peace, without getting smeared by over-excited little ones with Christmas-stocking melted chocolate money on their hands! Maybe for nostalgic reasons, at Christmastime I tend to be a bit of a traditionalist, so I love to do the whole turkey thing. But if I'm cooking for just a couple of people, I love a wonderful Roast Duck, or the Gratin of Parsnips and Jerusalem Artichokes for vegetarians in the party.

Smoked Salmon Pâté

Serves about 12 people

This is a delicious pâté that makes a little smoked salmon go a long way. Left-over scraps of smoked salmon are perfect for it, and it will keep for a week in the fridge. I love it on crusty white or brown bread or crackers. It is also lovely served on little crostini for a party (page 41).

100 g (4 oz) good smoked salmon
50 g (2 oz) cream cheese
150 g (6 oz) crème fraîche
1 tbsp lemon juice
pepper, and a tiny pinch of salt
1 tsp chopped fennel — optional

In a food processor, whiz up the smoked salmon, then add the cream cheese and the crème fraîche. Empty into a bowl and fold in the lemon juice, salt (you might not need any), pepper and chopped fennel, if using.

NOTE Sometimes I fry 50 g (2 oz) sliced or chopped smoked salmon in ½ tsp butter for 1 minute, till it is cooked; put it on a plate to cool. When it's cool, I flake it up with a fork and fold it into the pâté. This makes a really good, slightly rustic Smoked Salmon Pâté.

Smoked Trout and Avocado

Serves 6

This is one of Rory O'Connell's recipes and I love it. It is a fabulous starter or even a light lunch, at any time of the year.

2 fillets of smoked trout (about 175 g (6 oz))
1 x diced ripe avocado (¾ cm (¼ in) cube)
25 ml (1 fl oz) Mayonnaise (page 6)
1 tbsp French Dressing (page 4)
2 tbsp finely chopped scallions
salt and pepper
squeeze of lemon juice to taste

Flake the trout with a fork on a plate. Put into a bowl and add the diced ripe avocado and the chopped scallion. In a small bowl, mix the mayonnaise with the French dressing and add just enough to coat the trout and avocado lightly — do this very gently. Season with salt and pepper to taste. If necessary, add a small squeeze of lemon juice.

to serve:
There are a few ways to serve this — for Christmas dinner, you could place a 6 or 7 cm (2½ in) biscuit cutter on a plate (do 1 plate at a time) and spoon in enough smoked trout and avocado to come up about 2½ cm (1 in). Compress with a spoon, then gently lift the cutter off the plate, leaving a very 'chef-y' timbale of smoked trout and avocado on the plate. Decorate with a couple of flat parsley leaves.

Sometimes I like to make this 'timbale' on a bed of salad leaves on the plate. Or if it is for a casual lunch, you could just drop a large tablespoonful of the smoked trout and avocado on lettuce leaves on the plate. Or, of course, it would look lovely served in a bowl.

NOTE If you don't have any cutters to do the timbale thing, take a round, plastic, half-litre water or mineral bottle and cut it across to get about 4 timbale moulds, each about 5 cm (2 in) high. Of course, these are just for shaping — remove before serving. You can also use these again and again.

NOTE For a drinks party, spoon heaped teaspoonfuls of this mixture onto chicory or Belgian endive leaves.

French Dressing

A basic French dressing is made with 3 parts oil to 1 part vinegar. You will need only a tiny bit of this for the Smoked Trout and Avocado, but if you want to have some left over, make this amount — if not, just scale the recipe down to a quarter.

6 tbsp olive oil (use your best extra virgin for this)
2 tbsp white wine vinegar
1 tsp Dijon mustard
1 small clove garlic
sprig of parsley
a few chives or ¼ tsp spring onion
salt and pepper

Whiz up all the ingredients and season to taste. A good way to taste this is to dip a lettuce leaf into it, and see how it is.

Homemade Mayonnaise

Makes 300 ml (10½ fl oz)

2 egg yolks
½ tsp Dijon mustard
1 dessertspoon white wine vinegar
good pinch salt
25 ml (1 fl oz) extra virgin olive oil, combined with
175 ml (7 fl oz) sunflower oil

Put the egg yolks into a glass bowl. Add the salt, mustard and vinegar, and mix. Gradually add the oil, drop by drop, whisking all the time. You should start to see the mixture thickening. Keep adding the oil as you whisk until there is no more oil left. Season to taste. It should be smooth and creamy in texture. I usually make this with an electric hand blender with the whisk attachment. Made in seconds.

NOTE If you add the oil too quickly, the mixture will split – that is, it will look very thin and have a layer of oil floating on top. To rectify this, break another egg yolk, place in a clean bowl, and pour the 'split' mixture on, drop by drop, whisking all the time until it emulsifies.

Chicory, Blue Cheese, Pecan and Cranberry Salad

Serves 4

This is a very easy salad that my friend Alison makes. The flavours and textures are delicious.

225 g (8 oz) Cashel Blue cheese, cut into small cubes
1 head chicory
a selection of salad leaves
2 tbsp dried cranberries, chopped very roughly
12 pecans

dressing:
3 tbsp hazelnut or walnut oil
1½ tbsp white wine vinegar
¼ tsp Dijon mustard
salt and black pepper to season

Mix all the ingredients for the dressing together in a jam jar. Toast the pecans on a baking tray at 180°C/350°F/gas 4 for 5–10 minutes — don't leave them as they burn easily. When cool, chop or crumble them roughly. Trim the chicory and separate the leaves. Combine the cheese, nuts and cranberries in a bowl and toss with a little dressing. To assemble salad, choose a good mix of small salad leaves. Add some chicory and dressing. Add the cheese, nuts and cranberries.

NOTE For canapés, the cheese, nut and cranberry mixture can be sparingly spooned into the small chicory leaves.

See photo between page 16 and 17.

Roast Turkey

The method of cooking any bird (be it chicken, pheasant, guinea fowl or turkey) breast-side down for most of the time leaves it with meat that is juicy and tender. This stuffing has smoky bacon in it which is yummy, but you can, of course, leave it out.

1 x good-quality free-range turkey
25 g (1 oz) butter

1 x recipe for Stuffing (page 9) Make sure the stuffing is cold before you use it

Preheat the oven to 200°C/400°F/gas 6. Remove the wishbone from the neck end of the turkey — this makes carving the breast easier later — and remove the wing tips too. If you want to make a stock for your gravy, place into a saucepan the wishbone, wing tips, neck, heart and gizzard — but not the liver (that might be inside the carcass) — 1 carrot and 1 onion cut in half, a stick of celery, if you have it, and a sprig of thyme and parsley. Add a pinch of salt and cover with cold water. Simmer for 2 hours while the bird is roasting. Or you can make the stock in advance.

Wipe clean and dry the cavity of the turkey. Half fill with the cold stuffing and put the remainder of the stuffing in at the neck end. Weigh the turkey and calculate the cooking time. Allow 15 minutes per lb (or 33 minutes per kg) plus 15 minutes extra.

Smear the butter on the turkey and then place it, breast-side down, in the roasting tin (this prevents the breast from drying out) and roast for 20 minutes, then turn the oven down to 180°C/350°F/gas 4. About 30 minutes before the end of cooking time, turn the turkey breast-side up, basting it well with the juices in the tin — this will allow it to brown. At the end of cooking time, test to see if it is cooked (stick a skewer into the thigh of the turkey — the juices should run clear). Take it out of the oven, cover it with tin foil and place it somewhere slightly warm, if possible, while it rests.

I usually write down all these times, calculations, etc! Keep in mind that the turkey should 'rest' for at least 20 minutes after it has cooked, before you carve it. See below for the gravy recipe.

To carve a turkey, duck, chicken, goose — or any bird – allow it to rest for at least 10 minutes in a warm place before carving. If possible, place on a board sitting in a roasting tray – this will catch the juices, which can be added to the gravy. Holding the turkey steady with a carving fork, cut down through the skin between the breast and the leg. Cut through the ball and socket joint to remove the leg. Divide the thigh from the drumstick by cutting through the joint holding them together. The leg is the brown meat. For a turkey, you might want to cut the thigh into 4 or so pieces — to divide the brown meat. Remove the wish bone (at the neck end) if you have not already done so. Carve the wing off on its own, or carve some of the breast with the wing attached to it. Carve the remainder of the breasts (white meat) into slices and place, with the legs, in a warm serving dish. It always looks nicer if the meat is served skin-side up. Cover to prevent it from drying out, and keep warm until serving.

Gravy

When the bird (duck/turkey) is cooked, remove to a dish or another baking tray and keep warm. Pour off the fat from the tray, but not the bitty juices at the bottom. Pour boiling stock into the juices in the tray (about 400 ml (14 fl oz) for a chicken or a duck and about 800 ml (1½ pt) for a turkey) and whisk to remove and dissolve all the bits. If you have room on your hob, you can do this on a low heat. Strain into a saucepan and boil for a few minutes. Sometimes I add a sprig of whatever herb I'm using in the stuffing. Season with salt and pepper to taste. To thicken the gravy, make a roux by melting, in a small saucepan, equal quantities of butter and flour (say 25 g (1 oz) of each). Cook on a medium heat for 2 minutes. Then whisk a couple of tea-spoonfuls of this into the boiling gravy, while still on the heat. It will thicken as it boils.

Fresh Herb Stuffing with Smoky Bacon

This will stuff a good 5.5–6.75 Kg (12–15 lb) turkey

175 g (6 oz) butter
350 g (12 oz) onions, finely chopped
400 g (14 oz) soft white breadcrumbs
4 generous tbsp of chopped fresh herbs, like marjoram, tarragon, pars-
ley, thyme, chives, lemon balm, savoury, rosemary (rosemary is quite
strong so don't use too much)
150 g (5 oz) smoky bacon (I love Gubbeen bacon) cut into lardons
2 cm by ½ cm (¾ x ⅕ in)
salt and pepper

Place the lardons in a saucepan of cold water. Bring to the boil, drain and dry the bacon on kitchen paper. Heat up a frying pan. Add 1 tsp olive oil and, on a high heat, cook it (3–5 minutes) until golden and crispy.

Heat the butter in a pan. On a gentle heat, cook the onion (with a lid on) for about 8–10 minutes, until soft. Add the breadcrumbs, herbs and bacon, and season with salt and pepper to taste. Allow to cool completely before you stuff the bird, unless the bird is going straight into the oven.

A few points
- It is perfectly safe to stuff your bird — besides, you get a much better stuffing if it is cooked in the bird.
- Do not over-stuff the cavity — leave a little gap in the cavity to allow the heat to penetrate, so that the bird can cook completely.
- Do not put warm stuffing into a bird — allow it to cool before placing it in the bird, unless you put it in the oven straightaway. It's very handy to make the stuffing ahead of time. And of course you can freeze it.

Roast Duck with Sage and Onion Stuffing

Serves 4

Duck makes a very good alternative to turkey at Christmastime. In fact, many people tend to cook it only during the festive season, as it is not the cheapest bird around, but it is wonderfully rich and full of flavour.

Many people don't roast duck very often because they find that the oven gets very smoky, as duck is indeed very fatty. I find a very good way to combat this is to boil the duck first to remove excess fat.

1 x duck, about 2.2 kg (4¾ lb) in weight
1 tbsp olive oil
½ tsp sea salt
1–2 tbsp finely chopped sage

1 x recipe for Sage and Onion Stuffing (page 11). Make sure that the stuffing is cold before you use it.

Remove any loose fat, giblets and neck from inside the cavity of the duck. Using a small sharp knife, remove the wishbone from the duck to make carving easier later — this can be found at the end of the duck, at the entrance of the cavity, in between the two wings.

Place the whole duck in a large saucepan, and cover with cold water. Bring to a simmer, and continue to simmer for 30 minutes. Preheat an oven to 200°C/400°F/gas 6. Remove the duck from the saucepan, and briefly place on a wire rack to dry. With kitchen paper, pat the duck dry. Into the cavity, spoon the stuffing, not packing it too tightly in — this will alter cooking times. Make a few small, very shallow (only through the skin) incisions, with a knife along the breast and legs (or stab all over with a skewer). Into a small bowl, pour the olive oil, adding the salt and chopped sage, and mixing to make a paste. Rub this into the now-dry skin of the duck, pressing it into the incisions. Place the duck on a dry wire rack sitting on top of a roasting tray (if you don't have a wire rack, you could use a 'trivet' of spoons instead). Place in the centre of the preheated oven, and cook for 40–55 minutes, depending on the size of the bird. When it is cooked, the leg should feel slightly 'loose' on the bird, and a metal skewer when stuck into the thigh should come out too hot to place on the inside of your wrist!

NOTE See Gravy recipe (page 8).

NOTE See page 8 for tips on how to carve the duck.

Sage and Onion Stuffing

For 1 duck or chicken — serves 4–6

While the duck is 'boiling', you can make the stuffing. You can replace the sage with either thyme or rosemary.

35 g (1½ oz) butter
75 g (3 oz) (1 small) onion, finely chopped
100 g (4 oz) soft white breadcrumbs
1 tbsp chopped fresh sage
salt and pepper

Heat the butter in a pan, on a gentle heat. Add the onion and cook for about 8–10 minutes or until soft, with the lid on. Add the breadcrumbs and sage, and season with salt and pepper to taste. Allow to cool completely before you stuff the bird, unless the duck is going straight into the oven.

Brussels Sprouts

Serves 6

These little miniature cabbages from Belgium are actually really good if they are not completely overcooked. We always cut them in half at the cookery school and it works well as they cook quickly and evenly.

500 g (17½ oz) Brussels sprouts, with outer leaves trimmed,
and cut in half lengthways
600 ml (21 fl oz) water
1 tsp salt
25 g (1 oz) butter
pepper

Prepare the sprouts. Bring the water and salt to the boil, then add the sprouts, and cover with a lid until the water comes back up to the boil. Uncover and cook for about 5 minutes, or until the sprouts are just tender. Drain. Add butter and melt with the sprouts. Add pepper to taste and serve.

Brussels Sprout Mash

Serves 6

This recipe is very handy if you overcook the Brussels sprouts –
actually, it is so good that I often make it especially! If you are making
this in advance, just heat it up briskly in an uncovered pot — prolonged
covered heat will make it go dull in colour.

500 g (17½ oz) Brussels sprouts
75 ml (3 fl oz) cream
25 g (1 oz) butter
pepper

Cook the sprouts as in the Brussels Sprouts recipe (page12), drain
them, then whiz them in a food processor with cream, butter and a
good pinch of pepper.

Maple Roast Parsnips

Serves 6

The maple syrup in this recipe gives the parsnips a sweet subtle flavour. These are delicious with roast chicken too!

500 g (17½ oz) parsnips (4 large or 8 small), peeled, quartered with the woody root in the centre cut out, and sliced into long, even chunks
scant 50 ml (2 fl oz) maple syrup
pinch sea salt
2 tbsp olive oil

Preheat oven to 230ºC/450ºF/gas 8. Place the prepared parsnips in a saucepan of boiling water on the heat and boil for 3 minutes. Drain and dry in kitchen paper. (I find that this blanching gives the parsnips a lovely texture.) Toss in a bowl with the maple syrup and a pinch of sea salt. Drizzle the olive oil over, toss and empty out onto a roasting/baking tray (can be prepared up to this point). Place in the oven and roast for 15–20 minutes, or until golden brown and soft.

Potato and Jerusalem Artichoke Mash

Serves 6

The Jerusalem artichoke goes very well with duck. You can make this as rich as you like, adding milk or cream — see below.

500 g (17½ oz) Jerusalem artichokes, peeled
500 g (17½ oz) potatoes, peeled
25 g (1 oz) butter
50 ml (2 fl oz) milk, or if this is for Christmas dinner, cream!
2 tbsp chopped parsley
salt and pepper

In a saucepan of slightly salted water, place the peeled potatoes and boil for 10 minutes, then add the artichokes to the potatoes and continue boiling for another 15 minutes, or until both vegetables are nice and soft. Drain and mash. Add the butter and some milk or cream — you may need to add a little extra. Season with salt and pepper. Add the parsley and serve.

This mash can be made in advance and heated up in a covered dish.

NOTE If preparing the artichokes a few minutes in advance, store them in a bowl of water with a squeeze of lemon juice as otherwise they go brown very quickly.

Bread Sauce

Serves 10–12

This is Darina's recipe for bread sauce. In my opinion, this and cranberry sauce are a must to serve with roast turkey at Christmas!

600 ml (21 fl oz) milk
100 g (4 oz) soft white breadcrumbs
2 onions, peeled, and each stuck with 6 cloves
50 g (2 oz) butter
salt and pepper, a pinch or so of each
2 good pinches of ground cloves
100 ml (3½ fl oz) cream

Preheat an oven to 170°C/325°F/gas 3. Place all the ingredients, except the cream, in a small saucepan and bring to the boil. Cover and place in the preheated oven for 30 minutes. Remove the onion and add the cream. This can be made in advance. If it is too thick, just add a little milk.

Cranberry Sauce with Orange

Serves 10

This sauce can be prepared ahead and kept in the fridge for a week. It could also be frozen.

340 g (12 oz) cranberries (1 bag)
Finely grated zest and juice of 2 oranges — keep separate
150 g (5 oz) light muscovado sugar

Put the cranberries (they can be frozen) and the orange juice into a small saucepan and cook on a low heat, with the lid on, stirring regularly for about 6 or 7 minutes, until the cranberries have burst completely. Take the saucepan off the heat and stir in the grated orange zest and the sugar.

Crostinis with Parma Ham, Goat's Cheese and Onion Jam (page 42)

Chicory, Blue Cheese, Pecan and Cranberry Salad (page 6)

Pan-grilled Scallops with Lemon Oil, Baby Spinach and Pine Nut Salad
(page 32)

Flirtinis (page 28)

Baby Orange Mince Pies (page 22)

Ballymaloe Cheese Fondue (page 36)

Apple Sauce

Serves 4

To serve with roast duck, pork or goose. Keeps for a few days —
freezes too!

1 very large cooking apple (400 g (14 oz), which will be 300 g (10½ oz)
less peel, etc.)
75 g (3 oz) sugar
1 tbsp water

Peel, de-core and chop the apple into large chunks. Put into a small
saucepan. Add the sugar and water and cook on a very low heat for
8 minutes or until the apple is soft and pulpy. Stir and taste.

NOTE To make apple crumble, just place this apple sauce in a shallow
pie dish, and top with the crumble mixture (see Peach and Strawberry
Crumble, page 81). Then bake as for Peach and Strawberry Crumble.

Gratin of Parsnips and Jerusalem Artichokes

Serves 6

This is a delicious vegetarian Christmas dish, served with some red cabbage and roast potatoes. But it is also very good with roast duck — or with turkey too, for that matter.

500 g (17½ oz) parsnips, peeled and sliced ½ cm (¼ in) thick
500 g (17½ oz) Jerusalem artichokes, peeled and sliced ½ cm (¼ in) thick
10 g (½ oz) butter, for greasing the dish
salt and pepper
250 ml (8¾ fl oz) cream
100 ml (3½ fl oz) milk
1 tbsp wholegrain mustard
75 g (3 oz) grated Gruyère or parmesan cheese
5 sprigs thyme

Preheat the oven to 200°C/400°F/gas 6. In a saucepan of boiling water with a pinch of salt, blanch the parsnip slices for about 4–5 minutes until just soft. Pull out the parsnips and put in the Jerusalem artichoke slices and blanch these till soft. Drain. Butter an ovenproof dish (30 cm x 20 cm (12 in x 8 in)) and in it place the blanched vegetables, arranging them slightly. Season with salt and pepper. In a saucepan, place the cream, milk and mustard. Bring to just under boiling point and pour the mixture over the parsnips and artichokes. The liquid should half cover the vegetables. Sprinkle with the grated cheese, and pop the sprigs of thyme on top. The dish can be prepared in advance to this point. Cook in the preheated oven for 25–35 minutes or until it is golden and bubbly. You can cover it with tin foil for the last 10 minutes or so if it is already brown enough.

NOTE If preparing the artichokes a few minutes in advance, store them in a bowl of water with a squeeze of lemon juice — otherwise, they go brown very quickly.

Red Cabbage

Serves 6–8

This goes so well with duck, goose and pork too. It can be made in advance – it can even be frozen.

450 g red cabbage (red drummond if possible)
450 g cooking apples (Bramley's seedling)
1 tbsp wine vinegar
120 ml (4¼ fl oz) or 2 cups water
1 level tsp salt
2 heaped tbsp sugar

Remove any damaged outer leaves form the cabbage. Examine and clean if necessary. Cut in quarters, remove the core and slice the cabbage finely across the grain. Put the vinegar, water, salt and sugar into a cast-iron casserole or stainless steel saucepan. Add the cabbage and bring to the boil.

Meanwhile, peel and core the apples and cut into quarters. Lay them on top of the cabbage, cover and continue to cook gently until the cabbage is tender — 30–50 minutes. Do not overcook or the colour and flavour will be ruined. Taste for seasoning and add more sugar if necessary. Serve in a warm serving dish.

NOTE Try to get red drummond cabbage as this variety gives the best results.

Baked Risotto with Butternut Squash, Blue Cheese and Toasted Walnuts

Serves 6, though you can halve the recipe, or cut it to one-third easily, for 2 or 3 people

This is a fabulous wintertime risotto — great for somebody who does not eat meat at Christmastime. I sometimes make it in a large gratin dish, but you could also serve this in individual gratin dishes, straight to the table.

1–1.25 litres (1¾–2¼ pt) vegetable stock
25 g (1 oz) butter
2 tbsp olive oil
1 onion, finely chopped
400 g (14 oz) risotto rice
1 glass (about 300 ml (10½ fl oz)) white wine
750 g (1½ lb) butternut squash (about 1 butternut squash), cut into 1 cm (½ in) cubes, all seeds and skin discarded — you will need to peel this with a knife
salt and pepper
1–2 tbsp chopped parsley
100 g (4 oz) blue cheese, such as Cashel Blue or stilton
50 g (2 oz) walnuts, roughly chopped, and toasted in a moderate oven for 5 minutes or until golden

First, bring the stock to the boil. Then turn down the heat and keep it at a low simmer. In a large saucepan, melt the butter. Add the olive oil and the onion, cover with a lid, and cook on a low heat till the onion is soft, but not coloured. Add the rice and stir over a medium heat for a minute. Add the glass of wine, and let it boil for a few minutes till the wine evaporates, then add the cubed butternut squash. Season with salt and pepper, and turn the heat down to medium low — it needs to stay at a steady simmer. Add a ladleful of the hot stock from the saucepan. Simmer till it has nearly evaporated, then add another ladleful, and so on for about another 20 minutes, till you have added all the stock. It should be the consistency of quite sloppy wet porridge, and the rice and butternut squash should be very nearly cooked.

Stir in the chopped parsley, and correct the seasoning. Don't make it too salty, as you still have the salty blue cheese to add in at the end. Transfer the almost-cooked risotto to a gratin dish, about 22 cm (8¾ in) square, or smaller for individual baked risottos. Set aside till you want to bake it in the oven. It can be prepared ahead to this point.

Preheat an oven to 200°C/400°F/gas 6. Cover the risotto with tin foil and bake for about 30 minutes, or until hot and bubbly, taking off the tin foil halfway through cooking. When it comes out of the oven, spoon the risotto onto hot plates, or leave in the gratin dish if you wish, crumble the blue cheese over the top, and scatter with the toasted walnuts.

Savoury Pastry

Make exactly as for Sweet Pastry (page 23), but omit the sugar. And I sometimes still use the lemon rind — for instance, if I'm making a fresh tomato and basil tart, or Crab and Coriander Tart (page 58).

Baby Orange Mince Pies

Makes 24 mini mince pies

These are very cute and the perfect size to hold in your hand while you have a glass of Glühwein (page 26) in the other.

For this I use a mini muffin tray. The pies freeze very well and if I were making lots of them before Christmas, I would freeze them raw and then cook on the day. But if you have them cooked, store in a box with a lid and warm them gently to serve.

1 x the Sweet Pastry recipe (page 23). In place of the lemon rind,
add the finely grated rind of 1 large orange, or 2 small oranges.
250 g (9 oz) mincemeat (just over half a jar)
2 tbsp Cointreau (optional but divine)

Preheat the oven to 200°C/400°F/gas 6. Roll pastry until it is ¼ cm (¹⁄₁₀ in) thick. Take off the top sheet of cling film and, using a 6 cm (2½ in) pastry cutter (fluted, if you like), cut out 24 circles for the bases. Then use a 4 cm (1½ in) cutter (fluted again, if you like) to cut out more circles for the lids. Or you could use a 3 cm (1¼ in) star cutter for the lids instead. Re-roll the trimmings if necessary. Line the base of the muffin tray with the 6 cm (2½ in) rounds. Mix mincemeat and Cointreau. Fill each base with a teaspoon of mincemeat and top with the 4 cm (1½ in) rounds or the stars. Brush the top of the mince pies with any left-over beaten egg from the pastry.

Bake for 10–13 minutes until pale golden. Cool for 5 minutes before removing from the tin, then dust with icing sugar to serve!

NOTE These are very pretty topped with crystallised orange peel – optional. To make crystallised orange peel, using a peeler, peel strips off 1 orange and cut the orange into 5 julienne slices. Place in a small saucepan and cover with cold water. Bring up to the boil, then drain and cover with cold water again. Boil for 4–5 minutes until the peel is soft, then drain. Put the peel back into the saucepan with 25 g (1 oz) sugar and 50 ml (2 fl oz) water. Heat slowly to allow the sugar to dissolve, then boil for 4–5 minutes until the peel looks shiny and candied. Drain, then toss in sugar (caster or granulated). This crystallised peel keeps in a sealed jar for weeks and looks very pretty and festive.

See photo between page 16 and 17.

Sweet Pastry

Makes 475 g (1 lb) of pastry, enough to line 1 x 28 cm (11 in) tin (with a little left over), or 2 x 20 cm (8 in) tins (best to have removable bases)

Pastry freezes perfectly when it's raw, so it's handy to have some in the freezer. I always make it in the food processor, but if you don't have one, you can make it by hand.

250 g (9 oz) plain flour
125 g (4½ oz) butter, diced and softened
75 g (3 oz) caster sugar
½–1 egg, beaten
grated zest of ½ lemon (optional — I don't add this in for the Chocolate Tart, page 153)

To make pastry:
In the food processor place the flour, butter, sugar and the lemon rind, if using. Whiz up for a few seconds, then add half the beaten egg, and continue whizzing. You might need to add a little more egg, but don't add too much — it should just come together. (If making this by hand, rub the butter into the flour, add the sugar and lemon rind, if using, then, with your hands, bring it together with the egg). With your hands, flatten out the ball of dough till it is about 3 cm (1¼ in) thick. Wrap or cover it, and place it in the fridge for at least 30 minutes (it will keep well for a couple of days in the fridge or, of course, it will freeze). If I'm in a hurry, I sometimes put it in the freezer for slightly less time.

To roll:

Take the pastry out of the fridge. Preheat your oven to 180°C/350°F/gas 4, and place the pastry between 2 sheets (bigger than your tart tin) of cling film. Using a rolling pin, roll it out until no thicker than ¼ cm (⅛ in) thick, and preferably even thinner. Make sure to keep it round, if the tin is round, and large enough to line the base and sides of the tin. Removing just the top layer of cling film, place the pastry upside down (cling-film side facing up) in the clean tart tin. Press the pastry into the edges, cling film still attached, and, using your thumb, 'cut' the pastry on the edge of the tin. At this stage, it should look quite neat. Remove the cling film and pop the pastry in the freezer for at least 10 minutes (it would keep for weeks like this in the freezer).

To bake blind:

Bake blind by lining the pastry with greaseproof/parchment paper when cold (leaving plenty to come up the sides). Fill with baking beans, or dried pulses (you can use these over and over), and bake for 15–20 minutes, until the pastry feels dry to the touch. Remove the paper and beans, brush with a little left-over beaten egg and return to the oven for 2 minutes. Take out of the oven, and set pastry aside in the tin while you prepare the filling. This can easily be made a day in advance, and covered until you need it. The reason for baking the pastry blind is to prevent the tart from getting a soggy base — so when making a tart with a 'custard' filling (as in eggs and milk or cream), it's essential. But for other tarts such as the Chocolate and Pear Tart (page 96), baking blind doesn't seem to be necessary.

NOTE If the pastry is completely frozen going into the oven, and is not in any way too wet, you can actually cook it without the paper and beans. But if the pastry is not frozen, or is too wet (i.e. with too much egg), it will fall down the sides of the tin while it is cooking.

NOTE Sometimes I use the finely grated rind of 1 orange. I would do this for Baby Orange Mince Pies (page 22) and Strawberry and Honey Mascarpone Tart (page 69). Sometimes I add a little lemon rind for a different flavour.

Mincemeat and Almond Shortbread

Makes 32 squares

I love having some of this in the house at Christmastime. It's great with a cup of coffee. You can also freeze some, or give some as presents.

125 g (4½ oz) caster sugar
250 g (9 oz) butter, softened
250 g (9 oz) flour (or 375 g (13½ oz) plain flour if you don't want to use almonds)
125 g (4½ oz) ground almonds
300 g (11 oz) mincemeat
50 g (2 oz) nibbed almonds

Preheat an oven to 180ºC/350ºF/gas 4. If you have a food processor, whiz up the sugar, butter, flour and almonds until the mixture comes together. If you don't have a food processor, cream the butter in a bowl, then add the sugar, flour and almonds and work with your hands until it all comes together. Either way, divide the dough in two. Place one half in the freezer in a flattish round, and press the other half into a 23 x 33 cm (9 x 13 in) swiss-roll tin. Then spread the mincemeat out thinly to cover the dough in the tin. Take the remaining dough out of the freezer and place between sheets of cling film. Roll into a rectangle the same size as the tin. Peel off one layer of the cling film, and place on the mincemeat, cling-film side facing up. Smooth it out and, with your thumb, cut off the excess dough from the edges. Peel off the cling film, and scatter with the nibbed almonds, pressing them ever so slightly into the dough. Place in the preheated oven and cook for 45–50 minutes, until it is a pale golden brown all over and cooked through. Allow to cool before cutting and removing the shortbread. Dust with icing sugar if you like.

Glühwein

Serves 6–8

There is nothing like a bit of Glühwein to get you into the Christmas spirit. Serve with Baby Orange Mince Pies (page 22) for a bit of festive entertaining.

1 bottle of red wine
100 g (4 oz) muscovado sugar
1 cinnamon stick, broken in two
4 cloves
pinch of ground nutmeg
½ orange, cut into 4 chunks
1 lemon, cut into 4 chunks
250 ml (8¾ fl oz) brandy — less or more if you prefer

to serve:
halved orange slices from the remaining ½ orange

Put the wine, sugar, cinnamon, cloves, nutmeg, orange and lemon into a saucepan. Heat very gently, stirring to dissolve the sugar. Keep on a very low heat — without boiling — for 5 minutes. Remove from the heat. Add the brandy and taste for sweetness. Pull out the orange and lemon chunks. Serve in glasses, each with a new slice of orange in it.

NOTE If you want to make a delicious non-alcoholic version of this, replace the red wine with good apple juice and leave out the brandy.

NOTE If you have some of this left over till the next day, add a little water to it when reheating, as it tends to get quite strong and sweet.

Romantic Dinner for Two

Cooking for an intimate dinner for two takes a little planning — there are a few elements to consider. Firstly, the food should not need a great deal of last-minute preparing: it won't be much fun or particularly romance-inducing for your partner (or prey) to have to sit alone at the table all night while you faff about in the kitchen! Secondly, the food can be rich, but don't serve huge portions, unless you plan to fall into a heavy sleep as soon as you have finished eating. Thirdly, the food needs to look good to eat — as in, you need to look good eating it — so trying to chew your way through a huge sirloin steak might not be the most sensual thing! Fourthly, beware of too many herbs in the food — as we all know, parsley in the teeth is not a good look!

Flirtini

Serves 2

This cocktail is fab — the name even does it for me! You will definitely be flirting after one of these.

6 strawberries or 12 raspberries
25 ml (1 fl oz) Cointreau
50 ml (1¾ fl oz) vodka
juice of ½ lime
50 ml (1¾ fl oz) pineapple juice, chilled
125 ml (4¼ fl oz) sparkling wine or champagne, chilled

to serve:
a strawberry or raspberry for garnish

Mash the strawberries or raspberries and put into two champagne or martini glasses. Mix the Cointreau, vodka, lime juice and pineapple juice. Add to the glass and top up with the sparkling wine.

See photo between page 16 and 17.

Parma-Wrapped Bread Sticks

These are great with a cocktail or a drink before dinner. Simply wrap one end of the bread stick with Parma or Serrano ham, place on a serving plate and serve.

Oysters with Ginger and Lime Butter

Serves 2

Oysters are the ultimate aphrodisiac and sensual food to eat. This is for somebody very special! Oysters are at their best when there is an 'R' in the month.

6 Pacific oysters, opened, see below
75 g (3 oz) butter
1 tsp grated ginger
juice of ¼–½ lime

Remove the oysters from their shells (see below) and put the shells into a warm oven to heat up. Melt the butter. Add the ginger, and simmer for half a minute. Add the oysters and their sieved juice, making sure that there is no shell. Simmer in the butter for a minute. Add the lime juice, then spoon one oyster with ginger and lime butter into each shell. Serve with a wedge of lime on the side.

NOTE When serving oysters, do not serve whiskey to drink, as the two together can give people a bad reaction.

To open an oyster
Place the oyster on a tea towel, flatter side up. If you are right handed, wrap your left hand in another cloth so that, if the knife slips, you don't get cut. Take your oyster knife (or even chisel) in your right hand (do everything the opposite way around if, like me, you are left handed!) At the narrow end of the top shell, there should be a slight crevice. Insert the blade, while holding the opposite end steady with your wrapped-up hand, and press and turn the knife, levering upwards. Insert a clean knife just under the top shell to cut the oyster away from the shell — it will suddenly free. Serve as soon as possible. If you're serving the oysters raw, they should be served within the hour, at best, with a

wedge of lemon or a splash of Tabasco. If you're cooking the oysters, as above, they can sit in the fridge for a couple of hours before you cook them.

Strawberries with Balsamic Vinegar

This is a little starter — very surprising in flavour and absolutely gorgeous. The strawberries need nothing else with them. Make when strawberries are in season.

Simply sprinkle sliced strawberries, or whole little strawberries, with a bit of balsamic vinegar — just enough to be able to recognise the flavour. Make sure that the strawberries have come to room temperature — not chilled out of the fridge. Serve in 2 little cups or glasses.

Green Goddess Salad

Serves 2

My friend Eddie makes this delicious variation on the Caesar Salad. If you are making this for just two people, you'll need to make twice the amount of the dressing required as it's tricky to halve, but just add mashed avocado to half the dressing as, with the avocado in, it is good for only one day. Keep the other half of the dressing for another day — it will keep for a week.

So, to half the Caesar dressing (page 60), add half a mashed avocado, and proceed as for the Caesar Salad.

Champagne Sorbet

Serves 4

This could not be more romance-inducing, but it is also divine for a smart dinner party. I would actually serve this as a starter, or a second course, but of course, you could also have it for dessert.

50 g (2 oz) caster sugar
50 ml (2 fl oz) water
200 ml (7 fl oz) sparkling wine or champagne
1 tbsp lemon juice

Place the sugar and water in a small saucepan. Heat up slowly, stirring to dissolve the sugar, then boil, not stirring, for 4 minutes, uncovered, until the syrup measures about 50 ml (2 fl oz). Cool. Add the sparkling wine and the lemon juice. Place in the freezer. Take out of the freezer twice while it is freezing, at 3-hour intervals, and whisk the mixture to break up the crystals. Serve a scoop per person in a little glass and, if you like, pour a further tablespoon of bubbly over the sorbet.

To get ahead — because on a romantic night for two, you don't want to be spending too long in the kitchen, trying to scoop sorbet — scoop the sorbet early in the day and store on a plate in the freezer.

NOTE If you happen to have an ice-cream machine (sorbetière), just freeze it in that, according to the manufacturer's instructions.

Pan-grilled Scallops with Lemon Oil, Baby Spinach and Pine Nut Salad

Serves 2 as a main course

Everything can be prepared for this ahead. Just pan-grill the scallops and dress the salad at the last moment.

8 scallops with their corals
1 tbsp olive oil
½ tsp finely grated lemon zest to sprinkle over the salad at the end
sea salt and pepper
75 g (3 oz) baby spinach
25 g (1 oz) pine nuts, toasted until golden on a dry frying pan or in the oven

dressing:
3 tbsp olive oil
1 tbsp lemon juice

If the scallops have been frozen, let them sit on kitchen paper, which will absorb any moisture. Wash the scallops and dry them. Cut off the corals and put them with the scallops. With your fingers, remove any brown membrane from around the scallops, then slice the scallops in half horizontally. Keep chilled till you want them.

To make the dressing:
Mix the 3 tablespoons of olive oil and the lemon juice in a bowl. Season with salt and freshly ground black pepper.

Place the spinach in a bowl and heat up a grill pan or a frying pan (non-stick is handy) on the hob until very hot, for the scallops. Drizzle the spinach leaves with just enough dressing to coat them lightly.

Place on the plates and have the toasted pine nuts and lemon zest ready to hand. Drizzle the scallops with 1 tablespoon of olive oil and toss, then season with a small pinch of salt and pepper. Place on the hot grill pan or frying pan and cook until golden on each side, about 2 minutes. Take the pan off the heat and transfer the scallops to sit on or beside the spinach. Sprinkle with the toasted pine nuts and the grated lemon zest and serve.

See photo between page 16 and 17.

Buckwheat Pancakes with Crème Fraîche and Caviar

Makes 6 large (tablespoon drops) or about 20 small (teaspoon drops) pancakes

Caviar is made by pickling the roe of, most commonly, the sturgeon fish. But common it is not, unfortunately! A bit less expensive is caviar of salmon and lumpfish. It has long been thought to be a powerful aphrodisiac. Replace it with smoked salmon if you like (see page 35).

for the pancakes:
75 g (3 oz) white flour
40 g (1½ oz) buckwheat flour
good pinch of salt
⅛ tsp baking powder
1 egg
scant 100 ml (3½ fl oz) milk

to serve:
75 g (3 oz) crème fraîche
3 tsp (about 10 g (½ oz)) caviar
1 tsp chopped chives

To make the pancakes, place the flours, salt and baking powder in a bowl. Into the centre, add the beaten egg and milk, and continue to whisk until the mixture is smooth. Heat a frying pan (non-stick is handy). With a piece of kitchen paper, wipe the pan with a tiny knob of butter — no need to do this if it is non-stick. Place tablespoonfuls of the pancake batter (for pancakes 8 cm-ish (3 in) round) onto the hot pan and cook for 1–2 minutes on each side till golden and firm in the centre. (For tiny pancakes 3 cm (1¼ in), use teaspoonfuls of the batter.) Don't let the pancakes burn — the heat should be at medium. Once all the pancakes are made, place them on individual plates or one big plate. Let them cool and add a blob of crème fraîche (1 tsp for the big ones and ½ tsp for the tiny ones), and top with a little bit of caviar on each one (about ¼ tsp!) Sprinkle with a few finely chopped chives and watch them disappear off the plate. Preferably ask your lover to feed these to you between sips of champagne . . . I wish!

NOTE You could double the recipe for the pancakes if there are more than two of you for dinner.

Buckwheat Pancakes with Crème Fraîche and Smoked Salmon

Make exactly as above, but replace the caviar with a small slice of smoked salmon. I would assemble these differently — place the slice of smoked salmon onto the pancake, and on top of that add a small blob of crème fraîche. Finish by sprinkling with chopped chives or finely diced red onions.

NOTE I often make these with all white flour and no buckwheat flour. Just use 115 g (4 oz) white flour.

Ballymaloe Cheese Fondue

Serves 2

For a fantastic evening, this is not a light dish, but it is a fun thing to eat — of course, if you drop the bread into the pot, you have to kiss the person on your right, or is it left? I would suggest eating this as a main course, with no starter. And just maybe Strawberries in Champagne to follow, or if it is a winter's night, some chocolate truffles. This is also great fun for a casual dinner party — and great as a family dinner too.

1 tbsp dry white wine (if you put too much wine in, it can curdle quite easily)
1 large or 2 small cloves of garlic, crushed or finely grated
2 tsp tomato chutney (I use Ballymaloe Country relish)
2 tsp chopped parsley
175 g (6 oz) grated cheddar cheese (I sometimes use half cheddar and half Gruyère cheese)

In a small bowl, mix the wine with the garlic, tomato chutney and parsley. Add into the grated cheese in a fondue pot, or a small saucepan (non-stick would be very handy). Just before serving, place over a low heat until the cheese just melts and begins to bubble — stir only the odd time, as over-stirring can cause it to curdle (I tend to swirl the pan to stir it). Put the pot over the fondue flame or somewhere warm, or just straight on a board on a table, and serve with warm baguette, broken into pieces or cubes of bread toasted in a hot oven or — for absolute twee and over-the-topness — heart-shaped croutons!

To make the croutons:
Do this in advance and just warm them up before eating. Cut slices of white bread about 1 cm (½ in) thick and, using a cutter (star, heart, etc.) or a knife, cut into shapes or cubes. Lay on a baking tray and toast in a hot oven for 2–3 minutes.

See photo between page 16 and page 17.

Little Pots of Passion

Serves 2

This is a mango and passion fruit fool basically, except that title wouldn't exactly evoke many romantic thoughts! This recipe would be great for a summer dinner party too.

½ mango, peeled and chopped
1 passion fruit, halved and scooped
up to 1 tbsp lime or lemon juice
up to 1 tbsp caster sugar
75 ml (3 fl oz) cream

Purée the mango and passion fruit (including the seeds) with the lime or lemon juice and sugar. Use a food processor for this (if you use a liquidiser, you will need to add the passion fruit after, as it breaks up the seeds). Place in the fridge while you whip the cream softly. Then fold the mango and passion fruit purée in gently, leaving it a little marbled. Leave it in the fridge until you want to serve it. This is also delicious with the little Jane's Biscuits on page 38.

Strawberries in Champagne with Heart-Shaped Biscuits

Needless to say, I would not serve these for pudding if I had already made Strawberries with Balsamic Vinegar (page 30) for the starter. You can, of course, add sliced peaches or nectarines to this gorgeous summertime treat. If you're not opening a bottle of fizz anyway, just use a nice white or rosé wine. Make sure it is Brut (dry). This recipe varies, depending on the sweetness of the strawberries, but for two people, I would halve, or quarter, about 20 smallish strawberries, dust with about 1 tbsp sieved icing sugar and drizzle with 1 tablespoon lemon juice. Place in the fridge in two little glasses until you are ready to serve, then top up with chilled bubbles!

Serve with heart-shaped Jane's biscuits (below) on the side, and, at the risk of scarring (or securing) the object of your affections forever, write a little message in chocolate on the biscuit.

Jane's Biscuits

150 g (6 oz) plain flour
100 g (4 oz) soft butter
50 g (2 oz) caster sugar

Preheat an oven to 180°C/350°F/gas 4. Put the flour into a mixing bowl. Rub in the soft butter, then add the sugar and bring the whole mixture together to form a stiff dough. Or you can whiz everything up briefly in a food processor. Roll out the dough to ½ cm (⅛ in) thickness and cut into shapes/hearts! Place carefully on a baking tray and cook in the oven for 6–10 minutes until pale golden. Allow to cool for 1 minute before placing on a wire rack to cool.

Party Food

When cooking for any party that you have pre-planned, it makes such a difference if you can prepare a lot of the food in advance; your friends have come to see you, so try not to spend all the time in the kitchen. A friend of mine is so clever — she gets to mingle a little while her younger cousin and friend (for some extra pocket money, of course) help to pass around big plates of gorgeous little bites. As you and your guests are probably going to be standing when eating this food, you need to make sure that it is easy to hold, and that it can be eaten in one or two mouthfuls. I love this kind of food — not only are the recipes in this chapter good for parties, but each also works well for a sit-down meal too.

Marinated Olives

This recipe is from my last book, *Rachel's Favourite Food*, because I feel that for party food, flavouring your own olives is easy, yet they can be so good. Make your own spiced or herbed olives by starting off with some really good black or green olives. I prefer to leave the stones in. Add some freshly ground spices. Fennel seeds, cumin seeds and coriander seeds all work well, either together or on their own. Add some chopped chilli or a pinch of dried chilli flakes and/or some chopped herbs, such as coriander, marjoram, oregano, rosemary, sage, parsley or thyme. Top up with a couple of glugs of good extra virgin olive oil and store in a kilner/jam jar or a tied plastic bag in the fridge, where they will keep easily for a month. Let them get to room temperature before you serve them.

Roast Nuts

Roast nuts take hardly any time to make and they are quite different from ready-roasted nuts that you buy. To see the recipe for Spiced Roasted Nuts, go to page 184.

Basically take a mixture of nuts, or only one type — whole almonds (I like the unpeeled ones), cashews, macadamias, hazelnuts — and toss them in a bowl with just enough olive oil to coat lightly. Add a pinch of sea salt, and lay them out in a single layer on a baking tray. Roast in an oven preheated to 180°C/350°F/gas 4 for 10–16 minutes, until golden and toasted.

Crostini

Use these with Smoked Salmon Pâté (page 2). For party food, they are good with Serrano ham, goat's cheese or Imam Bayildi (page 47).

Makes about 30–40

1 x long, thin baguette
olive oil

Cut the baguette into slices straight across (they will be small and round) or at an angle, ¾ cm (¼ in) thick. Place in a bowl and drizzle with enough olive oil to coat. Place in a single layer in a baking tray. Put into a hot oven (200°C/400°F/gas 6) to toast for about 5 minutes or until pale golden. Take out of the oven, and serve warm or at room temperature with the topping of your choice.

Crostini with Parma Ham, Goat's Cheese and Onion Jam

Serves 10–20

1 baguette
8–10 slices of Parma or Serrano ham
110–175 g (4–6 oz) soft goat's cheese (I like Ardsallagh)
2 fl oz (50 ml) olive oil
¼ x recipe Onion Jam (page 43)
rocket leaves

Preheat the oven to 200°C/400°F/gas 6. Cut the baguette into 1 cm (½ in) thick pieces, at an angle or straight across (it's best if the bread is a day or two old). Put the slices of bread into a big bowl, and drizzle generously with olive oil until all the bread is evenly coated.

Spread the bread out flat on a baking tray and place in the preheated oven for 9–15 minutes until pale golden brown. Take out of the oven, cool, and on each of the crostini, place a piece of Parma or Serrano ham and a blob of soft goat's cheese. Top with a teaspoonful of onion jam. This is good without the onion jam too, but it is divine with it!

Decorate with rocket leaves and serve.

See photo between page 16 and 17.

Onion Jam

Makes 450 ml (16 fl oz)

This recipe makes a large amount, but it is great to have some in the fridge. Wonderful with the goat's cheese and Serrano ham, it is also delicious with lamb chops, and fantastic with cheddar or Gruyère cheese and crackers with a slice of tomato, or even in a steak sandwich. We often make this in the cookery school to serve with meat pâtés. It keeps in the fridge for months. If you are serving it with chops, you can heat it up if you like.

675 g (1½ lb) onions
50 g (2 oz) butter
1 tsp salt
½ tsp pepper, freshly ground
150 g (5 oz) caster sugar
100 ml (3½ fl oz) sherry vinegar, or balsamic vinegar
250 ml (scant ½ pt) full-bodied red wine — doesn't matter if it has been sitting around for a few days
2 tbsp cassis (a blackcurrant liqueur, available at your supermarket, or off-licence)

Peel and slice the onions thinly. Melt the butter in the saucepan and hold your nerve until it becomes a deep nut-brown colour — this will give the onions a delicious rich flavour — but be careful not to let it burn. Toss in the onions and sugar. Add the salt and freshly ground pepper and stir well. Cover the saucepan and cook for 30 minutes over a gentle heat, keeping an eye on the onions and stirring from time to time with a wooden spatula.

Add the sherry or balsamic vinegar, red wine and cassis. Cook for a further 30 minutes uncovered, stirring regularly. This must cook very gently (but don't let it reduce too much).

NOTE A student at the cookery school once told me that when she could not find cassis, she used blackcurrant cordial with success.

Little Tortilla Chips with Pea Guacamole

Makes about 50!

We make this pea guacamole at the school, and I love it on these little baked tortilla chips with a blob of crème fraîche or yoghurt on top.

3 wheat-flour tortillas (about 20 cm (8 in) in diameter)
1½ tbsp olive oil
pinch of sea salt

To make the base for the pea guacamole, cut the tortillas into squares or circles (with a cutter) about 2½ cm (1 in) in diameter. Either deep fry till golden or bake in the oven. To bake, toss them with the olive oil and lay out flat on a baking tray, sprinkle with salt, and roast in the oven for about 3 minutes at 220°C/425°F/gas 7, till golden. These can be made in advance. They will crisp up as they cool.

guacamole:
450 g (1 lb) frozen peas
2 tbsp olive oil
2 tbsp lime or lemon juice
2 tbsp chopped coriander (leaves and stalks)
½–1 chilli, deseeded and chopped
½ tsp ground cumin
½ tsp ground coriander
salt to taste

to serve:
75 ml (3 fl oz) crème fraîche or Greek yoghurt

Bring to the boil a saucepan containing just 4 cm (1½ in) of water and a pinch of salt. Add the peas and cook for just a minute after the water comes back up to the boil. Drain and refresh under cold water for a few seconds. Place the drained peas in a food processor with the rest of the ingredients. Blend until almost smooth. Taste and correct the seasoning. Put into a bowl and cover till needed. Spoon about ½ tsp on baked or deep-fried tortilla chips and dollop a tiny bit of crème fraîche or Greek yoghurt on top. Top with a bit of coriander leaf and serve.

This can all be made ahead of time. Just assemble closer to the time to be served.

NOTE These little baked tortilla chips are fab. I often cut the tortilla into big wedges and sometimes I add a pinch of chilli pepper flakes or crushed cumin into the olive oil. Great for nibbling with drinks.

NOTE Instead of the pea guacamole, you could top with Tomato and Avocado Salsa (page 46).

Tomato and Avocado Salsa

Serves 4

I love lots of this scooped up with Chilli and Garlic Pitta Crisps (page 130) or Little Tortilla Chips (page 44). Like so many of these salads, it's just great with a pan-grilled chicken breast, or served with Roast Fish (page 64).

1 large or 2 small avocados, peeled and chopped into 1 cm (½ in) cubes
10 cherry tomatoes, quartered, or 2 large tomatoes, roughly chopped
1–2 tbsp chopped coriander, mint or parsley
½ red chilli, deseeded and finely chopped — optional
juice of ½–1 lime
2 tbsp olive oil
sea salt and pepper

Mix together all the ingredients gently. Season with salt and pepper to taste.

Serve this in a bowl surrounded by lots of Chilli and Garlic Pitta Crisps (page 130).

Imam Bayildi

Makes about 25–30 crostini

This great spiced aubergine is so versatile — delicious on top of crostini with a blob of crème fraîche, but fab too with grilled or barbecued lamb. The mixture is best if it can sit around for an hour or more to let the flavours develop and mingle.

3 medium aubergines (about 850 g (1¾ lb)), chopped into 2 cm (¾ in) cubes
50 ml (1¾ fl oz) olive oil
1 tbsp cumin seeds, ground
¾ tbsp coriander seeds, ground
¼ tsp ground cardamom seeds (from the green cardamom pod)
3 large cloves garlic, crushed or grated
450 g (1 lb) tomatoes, peeled and chopped, or 1 tin chopped tomatoes
salt and pepper
50 g (2 oz) sultanas
2 tbsp chopped mint, coriander or parsley

Boil the aubergines in water with 1 tsp salt for 5 minutes. This will prevent them from absorbing too much oil. Drain them completely. In a pan, heat a little olive oil. Add the spices and cook for about 10 to 20 seconds, being careful not to let them burn. Quickly add the garlic and aubergines and stir fry for a minute. Now add the tomatoes, salt and pepper, and sultanas, and cook uncovered until the tomatoes have softened and the mixture has thickened. Add the herbs. When ready to serve, spoon a little onto each of the Crostini (page 41) and add ½ tsp blob of crème fraîche and a leaf of mint or coriander.

NOTE To peel tomatoes easily, put into boiling water for 10–20 seconds, then remove and peel.

Greek Salad on Chicory Leaves

See recipe for Greek Salad (page 62)

Cut everything into mini dice (1 cm (½ in)) and spoon into individual chicory leaves for great canapés.

Spicy Lamb Meatballs with Mint Yoghurt

Makes 25–30

450 g (1 lb) minced lamb
1 tsp ground cumin
1 tsp ground coriander
crushed seeds from 3 green cardamom pods (1 pinch)
4 cloves of crushed or grated garlic
1 small egg, beaten
salt and pepper
2 tbsp olive oil

Preheat oven to 230°C/450°F/gas 8. Mix all the ingredients except the olive oil together. To taste for seasoning, fry off a tiny bit in a hot frying pan, and add more spices if necessary. With slightly wet hands, make little balls, slightly smaller than a walnut in a shell — about 2 cm (¾ in) diameter. Heat up the olive oil in a frying pan. Add the meatballs and toss over high heat to brown, then transfer to a hot oven (230°C/450°F/gas 8) for 10 minutes, still in the frying pan, if it can go in (if not, transfer to a roasting tray). When they are cooked, split one open to check that it's fully done. Put them on a plate, stick a cocktail stick in each and serve with a bowl of mint yoghurt in the centre.

NOTE These can be rolled into balls in the morning to get ahead. They can also be prepared raw and frozen, if you like.

Sweet Corn and Coriander Cakes with Tomato Salsa (page 50)

Spicy Lamb Meatballs with Mint Yoghurt (page 48)

Greek Salad (page 62)

Provençale Chicken (page 77)

Moroccan Chickpea Soup with Chilli and Garlic Pitta Crisps (pages 71 & 130)

Moroccan Chicken Tagine (page 75)

Granny's Roast Potatoes (page 94)

Mint Yoghurt

1 tub of thick Greek yoghurt
1 generous tbsp chopped mint
salt and pepper
juice of ¼–½ lemon

Mix all the ingredients, and season to taste. Can be prepared in advance.

Chicory/Belgian leaves work brilliantly as a receptacle for holding salads. You need just 1 heaped teaspoonful for each leaf. I would put practically any delicious salad into these leaves — for example:

Smoked Trout and Avocado (page 3)
Greek Salad (page 62)
Salad of Green Beans with Feta and Pine nuts (page 66). Cut the green beans into 2 cm (¾ in) lengths.
Salad of Chickpeas with Red Onion, Tomato and Feta (page 164)
Smoked Salmon Pâté (page 2)

See photo between page 48 and 49.

Sweet Corn and Coriander Cakes with Tomato Salsa and Crème Fraîche

Makes 6

I tasted something like this in Mexico though it never would have been made with tinned sweet corn there, but this is a fast, convenient version! These are delicious served warm or at room temperature.

1 x 285 g (10 oz) tin of sweet corn, drained, or of course, fresh sweet corn cut straight off the cobb
1 spring onion, chopped
1½ tbsp chopped coriander
1 egg, beaten
salt and pepper
50 g (2 oz) self-raising flour
2 tbsp olive oil

for the salsa:
200 g (7 oz) (2 or 3) ripe tomatoes
1 spring onion, chopped, or 1 tbsp chopped red onion
1 tbsp chopped coriander
salt, pepper and a pinch of sugar
1 dessertspoon (approx) lime or lemon juice

to serve:
3 tbsp crème fraîche

First, make the salsa. Mix all the ingredients in a bowl and season to taste.

In a food processor, whiz up the sweet corn, onion, coriander and egg, then add the flour and very briefly whiz till it comes together. Season with salt and pepper to taste. Heat the olive oil in a frying pan and drop in teaspoonfuls of the mixture. Cook on a medium heat for about 3 minutes on either side, until golden. Take off the heat and put on plates. Onto each plate put a spoonful of salsa, then a nice little dollop of crème fraîche and a coriander leaf on top!

NOTE You can make these ahead if you want to — just pop the sweet-corn cakes into a hot oven for a minute or two to heat up.

NOTE These are a great party food, but are also lovely made bigger (tablespoon-size drops of the mixture) and served for lunch.

See photo between page 48 and 49.

Sushi

DO NOT LOOK AT THE LENGTH OF THIS RECIPE AND TURN TO THE NEXT PAGE. I PROMISE IT IS WORTH MAKING!

I do realise that many people can just run out to their local Japanese to pick up some sushi in 2 seconds flat; but those of us who can't do that, yet have a serious passion for sushi, need to know how to make it. Anyway, it is actually quite fun to make. Proper sushi chefs train for many years, but Isaac, my husband, and I taught ourselves. It is great to serve for a party, and it is just so good for you — I find it very addictive! You can make the vinegared rice in advance, if you like — I find it still good the next day — though the assembled sushi is best eaten within a few hours.

There are two main types of sushi: nori-maki rolls, and nigiri. It looks like a bit of a palaver but I assure you, it is worth the effort. Once the rice has been cooked and cooled, all you have to do is assemble either the maki rolls or the nigiri. This includes raw fish, so it needs to be as fresh as possible (you should not get a strong smell of 'fish' from it).

Serves 6 approx for a main course. But makes 60–80 pieces, so will serve lots for a party!

1 x recipe of Vinegared Rice (see below)
10 sheets of nori seaweed (about 1 packet)

filling – the reason I suggest having everything 22 cm (8½ in) long is that this is the width of the nori seaweed, which we are using to roll around the fish and avocado/cucumber; but don't worry if it is not.

10 slices (approx.) very fresh tuna, salmon or sole, cut into strips ½ cm x 22 cm (¼ in x 8½ in) (if it is not possible to cut strips this long, just cut them as long as you can, and make up to 22 cm (8½ in) long with another piece) (or thin slices 4 cm (1½ in) long and 2 cm (¾ in) wide, for the nigiri sushi)

1 avocado sliced ½ cm (¼ in) thick, and as long as possible (or thin slices, as above for the nigiri sushi)
½ cucumber (22 cm (8½ in) long,) seeded and cut into ½ cm x 22 cm (¼ in x 8½ in) strips
sesame seeds — optional

accompaniments:
wasabi paste — about 2 tbsp. This is often called Japanese horseradish — seriously hot!
shoyu – Japanese soy sauce (e.g. Kikkoman)
pickled ginger — about 4 tbsp

bamboo mat for rolling — not essential

nori-maki
Place nori on the bamboo mat if you have one (otherwise just on a board). With damp hands, spread about 3 tbsp of the rice very thinly on it, leaving a strip (1 cm (½ in)) of nori bare at the end closest to you, and also at the end furthest away from you. Brush this strip with water. Place a slice of fish and avocado or cucumber across the nori at the end closest to you. With the help of the sushi mat, roll it as tightly as possible away from you; the wet nori at the end should bind the roll shut. With a damp, sharp knife, cut into 6 or 8 slices. Clean the knife after each cut for tidy slices. If you want to make it a few hours ahead of time, wrap the rolls in cling film and refrigerate until you are ready to serve, then slice up.

nigiri sushi
With your hands wet, make a little oval-shaped patty with 1 dessert-spoonful of vinegared rice. Put a thin slice (about 4 x 2 cm (1½ x ¾ in)) of salmon or avocado on top. Sometimes I put a TINY blob (size of a grain of rice) of the hot wasabi sauce on top of the rice, under the fish. Sometimes I toss some of the rice 'patty' in toasted sesame seeds first.

temari sushi
Take a piece of cling film (about 10 x 10 cm (4 x 4 in)). Place a leaf of coriander in the centre, then a square thin slice of fish (about 2 cm

(¾ in)) and 1 heaped teaspoonful of vinegared rice. Gather up the edges and twist into a ball. Remove from cling film onto a plate.

to serve:

Place a selection of sushi onto one big plate. Put a little blob of wasabi mustard — about the size of a small pea — on the plate, a little dish of Japanese soy sauce and a few slivers of pickled ginger.

to enjoy:

Put a tiny dot of wasabi on a piece of sushi, dip in soy sauce and eat with chop sticks (or your fingers!) The pickled ginger is enjoyed between mouthfuls as a palate cleanser.

Vinegared Rice for Sushi

Vinegared rice, or su-meshi is the basis for all sorts of sushi. Sushi rice is a short-grain rice, and is now easily available.

450 g (1 lb) sushi rice
600 ml (1 pt) of water
50 ml (1¾ fl oz) rice wine vinegar
1½ tbsp sugar
2½ tsp salt

Wash the rice in cold water a few times until the water runs clear. Drain well, and allow to sit for 10 minutes. Put the rice in a small saucepan. Add the water, cover with a lid and bring to the boil. Then cook in the same water for 10–15 minutes, until all the water has been absorbed and the rice is cooked. Do not stir while it is cooking. With the lid still on, take the saucepan off the heat and set aside for 10 minutes.

Mix the rice wine vinegar, sugar and salt together in a small bowl. Turn the rice out onto a clean roasting tray or big mixing bowl. While it's still hot, pour the vinegar mix over it and gently fold through the rice. Allow the rice to cool, preferably even fanning it to speed up the process! The rice must be cool before working with it. If you are storing this in the fridge, do not put it in uncovered or it will harden.

Sweet Things

Basically anything sweet or savoury can be reduced to miniature size and that's what's so much fun about cooking food for a party like this. You might even want to change the drink when you are ready to serve sweet cakes — switch to a sweet red (or white) dessert wine in tiny glasses, maybe. But it does tend to draw the party to a close — so you decide if this is a good thing or a bad thing!

Mini Butterfly Buns

Make miniature versions of the butterfly buns on page 209 using a mini-muffin tin and mini-muffin paper cases. They will take only 7 or 8 minutes to cook and it will make double the amount of the regular size.

Mini Chocolate Tarts

Use half the recipe for the Chocolate Tart (page 153) and use 2 shallow bun trays, or mince pie trays, or even shallow mini bun trays.

Roll the pastry very thinly, to about 2 mm (less than ⅛ in) thick. Cut into rounds to line the bases of the tins. Freeze the pastry (for about 1 hour) till frozen (this means that you don't have to use baking beans), then pop straight into a preheated oven at 180°C/350°F/gas 4, for about 8 minutes or till pale golden. Fill with chocolate tart filling and pop back into the oven for another 8 minutes or until they are just setting. Take out of the oven and allow to sit in the tins for 10 minutes before taking out. Dust with icing sugar and serve.

Summer Lunch

Summertime food for me is all about easy eating — fresh food bursting with sunny flavours; food that can be transported easily to a table outside if the sun suddenly shines; food that you can happily eat lots of without feeling sluggish and heavy. Make the most of all the wonderful ingredients in season now (ingredients that haven't had to fly halfway across the world), like the tomatoes and the basil, the herbs and the lettuces, the fish and the lamb, and the strawberries and raspberries.

Crab and Coriander Tart

1 x recipe of Savoury Pastry (page 21)

Follow the method and line a tin 27 cm, with 3 cm sides (10½ in with 1¼ in sides) or 30 cm with 2 cm sides (12 in with ¾ in sides) and bake blind

filling:
300 g (10½ oz) crab meat, fresh (or frozen will do too). This is equal to about 2 medium-sized crabs
3 eggs and 1 egg yolk
300 ml (10½ fl oz) cream
1 tbsp lemon juice
2 tbsp chopped coriander
1 tsp grated ginger
¼–½ red, deseeded chilli, chopped (taste — you may need to add more, or Tabasco — about ½ tsp)
salt and pepper
50 g (2 oz) grated parmesan

Preheat an oven to 180°C/350°F/gas 4. To cook a medium-sized crab, place it in a saucepan, cover with water, add 1 tsp salt and bring to the boil. Boil for 10 minutes then pour off ⅔ of the water and continue to cook the crab, with lid on, for another 6 minutes. Take out and allow to cool.

To extract the meat, remove the large claws, crack the shells (using a heavy weight), and extract every bit of meat using the handle of a teaspoon, discarding all of the shell. Turn the body of the crab upside down and pull out the centre portion. Discard the 'dead man's fingers' (the gills) — they look like soft little fingers 4 cm (1½ in) long — and scoop out all the lovely brown meat and add it to the claw white meat. You can freeze this.

Whisk the eggs and yolk. Add the rest of the ingredients, except the parmesan. Add salt and pepper to taste. Pour into the baked pastry in the tin, sprinkle with parmesan and bake for 40 minutes, until it feels firm to the touch in the centre.

NOTE Serve with Chunky Tomato Salsa (below) on the side.

Chunky Tomato Salsa
(to serve with the Crab and Coriander Tart)

This is another thing that is great with a barbecue.

Make as tomato salsa, for the Sweet Corn and Coriander Cakes with Tomato Salsa and Crème Fraîche (page 50), but cut the tomatoes into biggish chunks, 2 cm (¾ in) approx.

Caesar Salad

Serves 4–6

Another great recipe of my friend, Dervilla's. Feel free to add a sliced pan-grilled chicken breast, cubed crispy bacon or slices of avocado to this, or, as in the Green Goddess Salad (page 30), add some mashed avocado to the dressing. This will keep for about a week in the fridge.

1 head of cos (romaine) lettuce
2–3 slices of white bread, cut into 2 cm (¾ in) cubes
2 tbsp olive oil

dressing:
25g (1 oz) (½ a small tin) anchovy fillets, drained and crushed or finely chopped
1 egg yolk
1 small clove of crushed or grated garlic
1 tbsp lemon juice
pinch of English mustard powder or ¼ tsp English mustard
¼ tsp salt
½ tbsp Worcestershire sauce
1–2 tsp Tabasco sauce
75 ml (3 fl oz) sunflower oil
25 ml (1 fl oz) olive oil
25 ml (1 fl oz) (2 tbsp) water

to serve:
25–50 g (1–2 oz) coarsely grated parmesan cheese

Preheat the oven to 220°C/425°F/gas 7 for the croutons. Wash the leaves of lettuce, dry well and place in a bowl in the fridge while you make the croutons and dressing. To make the croutons, toss the cubed bread with the olive oil, place on a baking tray and toast in the oven for 4 to 5 minutes, or until golden. Or you can fry these in a pan on the hob. When cooked, place on kitchen paper.

To make the dressing, place the chopped or crushed anchovies in a bowl (or the bowl of a food processor). Add the egg yolk, garlic, lemon juice, mustard, salt, Worcestershire sauce and Tabasco sauce. Whisk everything together, then add the sunflower and olive oil very slowly, whisking all the time until all the oil is added and the mixture is emulsified. Whisk in the water, and season to taste (but it shouldn't need anything). Take the bowl of chilled crisp lettuce out of the fridge. Add the croutons, half the grated parmesan cheese and enough dressing to coat all the leaves lightly. Toss gently. Arrange the salad on one big plate or individual plates or shallow bowls, and sprinkle the remaining parmesan on top. Serve!

Greek Salad

Serves 4

This is the simplest salad, and is so delicious in summertime when the tomatoes and cucumbers are in season. It is best made just before you want to eat it or, at the very least, drizzle it with the dressing just before serving. I would often serve this with a chicken breast or lamb chop. It's great with a barbecue.

1 small red onion, finely sliced, or 3–4 spring onions
100 g (4 oz) feta cheese, broken into 2 cm (¾ in) chunks, drizzled with
1 tbsp olive oil, black pepper and 1 tsp chopped marjoram
½ fresh cucumber, cut into 2 cm (¾ in) chunks
4 tomatoes, cut into 2 cm (¾ in) chunks
2 tbsp extra virgin olive oil
¾ tbsp lemon juice
1 generous tbsp chopped marjoram, or, failing that, parsley
20 good black olives, such as Kalamata

Mix the feta with the olive oil, black pepper and chopped marjoram. This can be prepared a few hours in advance if you like — it will only improve in flavour.

Mix in a wide bowl the cucumber, tomatoes and onion. Season with salt, pepper and a pinch of sugar. In a small bowl, mix the 2 tbsp olive oil, lemon juice and marjoram, and drizzle over the cucumbers, tomatoes and onion. Scatter with the feta cheese and olives. Serve!

NOTE This is great inside a split, warmed pitta bread — first a small handful of shredded cos, then a big spoonful of Greek Salad and finally a blob of Greek yoghurt. It is also lovely with some crisp cos lettuce leaves as a base on the plate, or tossed through. Cut everything into mini dice (1 cm (½ in)) and spoon into individual chicory leaves for great canapés.

NOTE Sometimes, to make quite a substantial Greek Salad for lunch, I add about half a 400 g (14 oz) tin of drained haricot beans and toss them through.

See photo between page 48 and 49.

Greek Salad with Pan-grilled Chicken

Serves 4 as a main course or 8 as a starter

1 x recipe for Greek Salad (above)
4 chicken breasts, drizzled with 2 tbsp olive oil, a pinch of freshly ground black pepper and a sprig of marjoram. This can be prepared in advance and left to sit in a fridge for a few hours if you like.

to serve:
Heat a grill pan, or frying pan to very hot, with no oil. Add the chicken breasts, smooth side down first, and cook for 2–3 minutes until golden, then turn over. Season with a pinch of salt and place in a hot oven for 8 minutes, or until they are cooked through, or continue cooking on a low heat on the hob. While it is cooking, dress the Greek Salad. When the chicken breast is cooked, remove and place on plates with some Greek Salad on the side, and maybe a small bowl of Greek yoghurt on the table.

Variation — Slice the cooked, cooled chicken breast and add to the pitta sandwich as above.

NOTE It is best to cook the meat from room temperature — so remove from the fridge about 15 minutes before you want to cook it. Cover it while it is sitting out.

Lamb Chops with Greek Salad

Serves 4

4–8 lamb chops, depending on their size, cut 1½–2 cm (¾ in) thick
olive oil
a pinch of black pepper
1 whole sprig of marjoram

Drizzle the raw lamb chops with the olive oil, pepper and marjoram.

Cook on a very hot grill pan (or frying pan) for just about 3 minutes on either side. Serve with the Greek Salad (page 62) on the side. A bowl of Greek yoghurt in the centre of the table would be good too — a little dollop of it works well with the meat and the salad.

NOTE It is best to cook the meat from room temperature — so remove from the fridge about 15 minutes before you want to cook it. Cover it while it is sitting out.

Roast Fish with Lemon and Basil Potato Salad

Serves 4

The fish is browned on a grill pan, then the whole thing popped into a hot oven to roast, which gives you a lovely result.

Lemon and Basil Potato Salad
850 g (1¾ lb) new waxy potatoes
75 ml (3 fl oz) lemon juice (juice of 1 large lemon)
75 ml (3 fl oz) olive oil
sea salt and freshly ground black pepper

2 spring onions (scallions), finely sliced
3 tbsp shredded or torn basil leaves

4 x 175 g (6 oz) portions of filleted cod, hake, mullet or whole mackerel fillets. I normally leave the skin on for this — it will get nice and crispy.
1 tbsp olive oil

to serve:
wedges of lemon and basil leaves

Preheat the oven to 220°C/425°F/gas 7. In a saucepan of salted water, boil the potatoes for about 20 minutes, or until just cooked. Drain, peel the skins off, slice 1 cm (½ in) thick, and dress with the lemon juice and olive oil while still hot. Season with salt and pepper.

Place a grill pan on the heat. Drizzle the fish with 1 tbsp olive oil, salt and pepper and place on a smoking hot grill pan, flesh side down. Cook for a minute or so till it is golden on the bottom, then turn it over and transfer to a hot oven — still on the grill pan, or if you are cooking it on a pan that won't go in the oven, transfer it to a hot baking tray that has heated up in the oven. Cook for another 5–7 minutes, or until it has turned opaque in the centre. While it's cooking, add the spring onions and herbs to the potato salad and place on plates. Then put the fish on top, or beside it. Add a wedge of lemon and a couple of basil leaves, and serve.

NOTE I sometimes use mint or even coriander instead of the basil here.

NOTE If you are cooking mackerel, it will not need to go in the oven as it takes only about 2 minutes on either side in the pan on the hob.

Salad of Green Beans with Feta and Pine Nuts

Serves 6, or about 10 as part of a selection of salads

I love this fresh summery salad. It's good on its own, or as part of a few summery salads. It's also very good with some barbecued or pan-grilled lamb chops.

450 g (1 lb) green beans, topped and tailed
2 tbsp olive oil
finely grated zest and juice of ½ lemon
sea salt and freshly ground pepper
75 g (3 oz) pine nuts, toasted on a dry pan until golden . . . don't burn!
125 g (4½ oz) feta cheese

Cook the green beans in boiling water with ½ tsp salt for about 3 minutes, with no lid (take the lid off once the water comes back to the boil) — until they still have a bit of a bite. Drain them, and while they are still hot, drizzle over the olive oil. Add the lemon juice, zest and salt and pepper to taste. Next, add the toasted pine nuts, and crumble in the feta cheese. Toss the salad and serve while still warm, or at room temperature.

Steamed Mussels with Basil Cream

Serves 6

This recipe is inspired by a dish I adore eating at the fabulous Fishy Fishy Café in Kinsale.

2–5 kg (4½–11 lb) mussels (about 100 mussels)
150 ml (5¼ fl oz) cream
50 ml (1¾ fl oz) (3 very generous tbsp) basil pesto

Scrub the mussels very well and discard any that are open and do not close when tapped. Place the cream and the pesto in a large saucepan on the heat and bring to the boil. Add the mussels, cover with a lid and place on a medium heat. Cook the mussels in the pesto cream for about 5–8 minutes, or until all the mussels are completely open. Pour, with all the lovely creamy juice, into a big bowl, or 6 individual bowls, and serve. Place another bowl on the table for empty shells, and some finger bowls and plenty of napkins! Serve with some crusty white bread on the side.

NOTE Pull out any mussels that do not open during cooking.

Banana and Mango with Lime and Honey

Serves 4

This is great after a rich or spicy meal. It also makes a wonderful breakfast with Greek yoghurt or you can have it as a dessert with vanilla ice cream or a dollop of crème fraîche.

2 bananas, sliced at an angle ½ cm (¼ in) thick
1 mango, peeled and sliced ½ cm (¼ in) thick
juice and finely grated zest of 1 lime
1 generous dessertspoon of honey

In a bowl, mix the honey, lime zest and juice. Gently mix in the mango and banana. If making in advance, add the bananas just before serving.

Strawberry and Honey Mascarpone Tart

This is like the most divine strawberry shortcake, with a twist. Feel free to replace the strawberries with raspberries, blueberries or even a mixture of the three.

1 x recipe for Sweet Pastry (page 23), with the finely grated rind of 1 orange added in place of the lemon. Bake it blind and place out of the tin on a big serving plate.
150 ml (5¼ fl oz) cream
250 g (9 oz) mascarpone (1 x tub)
4 tbsp honey
2 tbsp orange juice or Cointreau
150 g (5 oz) strawberries, sliced. If using raspberries or blueberries instead, don't slice them.
1 x 27 cm (10½ in) tin with 3 cm (1¾ in) sides or 1 x 30 cm (12 in) tin with 2 cm (¾ in) sides

In a bowl, whisk the cream with the mascarpone and 2 tbsp honey until it is the consistency of whipped cream. Fold in the orange juice or Cointreau. Spread out in the cooled pastry case and arrange the strawberries on top. Brush with 2 tbsp of warmed honey to glaze the top.

See photo between page 112 and 113.

Midweek Supper Party

If you are having people over to your home during the week, chances are you have been out at work all day, or you have been busy trying to get children to bed, or maybe even both! So you need either food that can be made quickly with minimum fuss, or something that you have made the previous night, that still did not take hours to conjure up. This is lovely informal entertaining, to allow good friends to catch up with each other.

Moroccan Chickpea Soup

Serves 4–6

I love the zing of flavour from the lemon juice in this. Another great quick soup to make, it would be perfect to bring to work in a flask. I vary this recipe a lot — sometimes I add leeks instead of, or as well as, the celery; sometimes I add some chopped crispy bacon; sometimes a clove or two of garlic in with the onions.

3 tbsp olive oil
125 g (4½ oz) chopped onion (1 onion)
100 g (3½ oz) chopped celery (2 stalks of celery)
salt and pepper
2½ tsp freshly ground cumin
1 x 400 g (14 oz) tin chopped tomatoes
a big pinch of sugar, to sweeten the tomatoes
1 x 400 g (14 oz) tin chickpeas, drained
600 ml (1 pt) vegetable or light chicken stock
juice of ½ lemon
2 tbsp chopped coriander leaves and stalks

Heat the olive oil in a saucepan. Add the onions, celery, and some salt and pepper, and cook on a low heat with the lid on until soft but not coloured — about 10 minutes. Add the cumin and cook for another minute, then pour in the tomatoes and all their juice, the sugar, the chickpeas, and the stock. Simmer for 5 minutes, then add the lemon juice and chopped coriander. Season to taste, and serve.

NOTE Tinned chickpeas are great for making this soup in a hurry, but of course you can also use dried chick peas. Just weigh 150 g (5 oz) of dried chickpeas (equivalent to 400 g (14 oz) canned cooked), cover them in cold water and soak overnight. Drain and cover in fresh cold water the next day, and boil until cooked — about 20–30 minutes. Don't add salt while cooking, as this toughens the skin.

NOTE If you are using dried chickpeas and have forgotten to soak them overnight, place them in a saucepan, cover with cold water and bring to the boil. Boil for a minute, then drain and cover with fresh cold water. Simmer until cooked. It will take a little longer to cook the un-soaked chickpeas, but they will cook.

NOTE When buying canned beans, of any sort, try to avoid the cans that contain added salt.

See photo between page 48 and 49.

Chunky Smoked Haddock Chowder

Serves 6

This is such a good, comforting, warming soup, and it is really quite quick to make. Feel free to replace some of the smoked haddock with unsmoked fish if you like, and mussels and prawns are good in this too. Of course, this can be reheated, but if you want the smoked haddock to stay in nice chunks, don't boil it too vigorously and don't stir it too much.

25 g (1 oz) butter
100 g (3½ oz) sliced onion (1 small onion)
225 g (8 oz) sliced leeks (2 smallish leeks)
salt and pepper
250 g (9 oz) potatoes (3 medium potatoes), cut into 1 cm (½ in) dice
400 ml (14 fl oz) vegetable or light chicken stock
400 ml (14 fl oz) milk
400 g (14 oz) smoked haddock (1 medium fillet), preferably un-dyed, cut into 2 cm (¾ in) chunks
25 ml (1 fl oz) cream – optional
2 tbsp chopped parsley

In a saucepan, melt the butter. Add the onions and leeks, season with salt and pepper, and sweat over a gentle heat until soft but not coloured — about 10 minutes. Add the potatoes, stock and milk; bring to the boil and simmer for 10 minutes or until the potatoes are just cooked. Add the smoked haddock and continue to simmer for 2 or 3 minutes until the fish is just cooked. Season again if necessary. Stir in the cream and chopped parsley, and serve.

Couscous with Lemon and Mint (or Coriander)

Serves 4–6

Couscous is a staple food in North Africa. The couscous that is available here is precooked and instant, so it is incredibly quick to prepare.

500 ml (17½ fl oz) medium couscous
4 tbsp olive oil
juice of 1 lemon
500 ml (17½ fl oz) boiling chicken stock or water
salt and pepper
3 tbsp chopped mint or coriander, or just parsley

Place the couscous in a bowl, add the olive oil and the lemon juice, and mix well to coat the grains. Pour in the boiling stock or water, and season with salt and pepper. Cover and allow to sit in a warm place until all the liquid has been absorbed — about 5–10 minutes. Stir in the chopped herbs, and serve.

NOTE Couscous is served very easily and looks quite tidy if you place it in a slightly wet tea cup, press it in a bit, and turn it out onto your serving plate.

NOTE Add the chopped herbs into this just before serving. Otherwise they will go very dull.

See photo between page 144 and 145.

Moroccan Chicken Tagine

Serves 4–6

A tagine is a Moroccan/North African 'stew' which is traditionally cooked in a conical vessel called a tagine. This is my own version of a tagine, cooked in a roasting tray in the oven. Like many others, it contains honey to give it a wonderful sweetness. I like to serve this with Coriander Couscous (page 74). For convenience, you can of course make the sauce for this in advance, then add the chicken half an hour or so before you would like to serve the tagine.

1 chicken, about 1.5-2.25 kg (3¼–5 lb), jointed and skinned, or about 6 large chicken breasts
4 tbsp olive oil
4 cloves of garlic, crushed or grated
2 onions, chopped (about 250 g (9 oz))
2 tsp grated ginger
1½–2 tbsp coriander seeds, crushed
3 tsp cumin seeds, crushed
1½ tsp ground cinnamon
salt and pepper
1 tbsp tomato paste
1 kg (2¼ lb) nice ripe tomatoes, coarsely chopped, or 2 tins of tomatoes
2-3 tbsp honey

to serve:
wedges of lime or lemon, and a bowl of Greek yoghurt

Heat up a saucepan. Add the olive oil, garlic, onions, ginger, and the spices. Season with salt and pepper. Stir, and then cook on a low heat with the lid on for about 10 minutes until the onions are soft. Add the tomato paste, the chopped tomatoes, and the honey, and continue to cook, this time uncovered, till the tomato sauce is quite thick — about 20 minutes — stirring every now and then. Season to taste; the flavour should be quite sweet and flowery. If you are using a big, wide-ish pan that will fit all the chicken pieces in a more or less single layer, add them to the pan, covering them in the sauce, and cook with the lid on, on a low heat, stirring every so often, for about 25 minutes until the chicken is cooked. If you don't have a big, wide pan, place the chicken pieces in a roasting tray, cover with the sauce and cook in an oven at 180°C/350°F/gas 4 for about 30–40 minutes till the chicken is cooked.

To serve, place the chicken on serving plates, with a wedge of lime or lemon on the side, some couscous with mint (page 74), and a bowl of Greek yoghurt in the middle of the table.

NOTE If you want to prepare this in advance, which will be really good for the flavour, you could make the tomato sauce completely, let it cool (this is important), and toss the raw chicken pieces in it, then cover and put it in the fridge. While it is waiting for you, it will be marinating and even improving in flavour. Do this up to 24 hours in advance.

NOTE Sometimes I make this in the traditional Moroccan way — I leave the chicken whole and cook it in the sauce (as with the pieces) but I put it into an oven in a covered saucepan at 160°C/325°F/gas 3 for about 1½ hours or until cooked. Then the chicken is brought whole to the table, and the meat is taken off the carcass, shredded into pieces, and served with the sauce.

See photo between page 48 and 49.

Provençale Chicken

Serves 4–6

*1 chicken, about 1.5-2.25 kg (3¼–5 lb), jointed and skinned (see below),
or about 6 large chicken breasts*
3 tbsp olive oil
2 red onions, sliced
3 cloves of crushed or grated garlic
good pinch of salt and pepper
1 tsp sugar
1 x 400 g (14 oz) tin of chopped tomatoes
2 tbsp chopped herbs — a mixture of basil and marjoram
1 glass (150 ml (5 fl oz)) white wine
*20 olives, chopped roughly (bash the olives to stone them, then throw
out the stones)*
25 g (1 oz) capers (rinse them if they are in salt)
1 x 55 g (2 oz) tin anchovies (about 12 fillets), roughly chopped
1 tbsp lemon juice
1–2 tbsp chopped herbs, to add in at end

Preheat the oven to 180°C/350°F/gas 4. Heat the olive oil, add the
onions and garlic, and season with salt, pepper and sugar (this will help
the tomatoes). Cover and sweat on a gentle heat until soft — about 10
minutes. Add the tomatoes, herbs, wine, olives, capers and anchovies,
and cook for another 20 minutes uncovered, or until the sauce has
reduced to a nice thick purée; stir regularly to prevent it from burning.
Taste and adjust the seasoning. While the tomato sauce is cooking,
brown the chicken pieces in a drizzle of olive oil, in batches, in a frying
pan over a high heat. Place the chicken in a gratin dish, roasting tray, or
wide sauté pan, and cover with the sauce. Cover with tin foil or a lid and
place in the preheated oven. Cook for 40 minutes, or until the chicken is
tender and cooked through. When it's cooked, stir through the lemon
juice, and another 1–2 tbsp chopped herbs, and serve.

See photo between page 48 and 49.

Provençale Fish

As above, but replace the chicken with 6 x 150g (5 oz) portions of a good fresh round fish like cod, haddock, whiting, salmon, ling or hake. If the fish portions are rather thin, fold them in two, so that they resemble thicker pieces of fish. I like to brown the fish first, very briefly, in a non-stick frying pan with a little olive oil (like the chicken, above), but that's not essential — it just gives it a nice golden colour.

The fish, provided that it is about 3 cm (1¼ in) thick, will take about 15 minutes to cook. It should feel firm in the centre when it is cooked; or you can stick a knife in one of the portions to make sure.

Baked Potatoes with Sea Salt and Thyme

Serves 4–6

Quick and easy — throw into the oven to serve with the Provençale Fish or Chicken.

450 g (1 lb) potatoes, with skin on (new spuds are good too)
2 tbsp olive oil
a big pinch sea salt
2 sprigs of thyme (or rosemary)

Preheat the oven to 230°C/450°F/gas 8. If the potatoes are large, cut them in half. Toss them with olive oil and sprinkle with sea salt. Pop on a baking tray and add the thyme sprigs. Cook in the preheated oven for 30 minutes, or until soft.

Penne Pasta with Aubergine, Basil and Pine Nuts

Serves 4–6

25 ml (1 fl oz) olive oil
350 g (12 oz) aubergines, cut into 1 cm (½ in) dice
4 cloves of crushed or grated garlic
2 tbsp tomato purée mixed with 2 tbsp water
2 tbsp torn basil
salt and pepper and a pinch of sugar

500 g penne pasta
olive oil to drizzle on cooked pasta

to serve:
50 g (2 oz) lightly toasted pine nuts
2 tbsp shredded or torn basil leaves
25 g (1 oz) grated parmesan

To make the sauce, heat the oil in a frying pan, add the diced aubergine and garlic and cook on a high heat till golden — about 5 minutes. Add the tomato purée mixed with the water, salt, pepper, pinch of sugar and the 2 tablespoons of shredded or torn basil. Lower the heat and cook until the aubergine is soft. Add more water if the aubergine sticks.

Put the pasta on to cook in a large pot of boiling water with 1 tsp salt. Cook for 7 or 8 minutes, or until just cooked. Drain, drizzle with olive oil, and add the sauce. Toss to coat the pasta. Sprinkle with pine nuts and the basil and grated parmesan, and serve immediately.

Caramel Poached Peaches

Serves 4–6

The caramel gives the peaches such a delicious flavour. Sometimes I add other fruit to this when it has cooled down — like raspberries or blueberries, or sliced bananas.

200 g (7 oz) sugar
100 ml (3½ fl oz) cold water
200 ml (7 fl oz) hot water
a few strips of lemon zest, removed from ½ lemon, with a peeler
4 peaches, or nectarines, cut in half, and stoned
juice of ½ lemon

In a saucepan, place the sugar and cold water, and stir over a low heat until the sugar dissolves. Then remove the wooden spoon, turn up the heat and boil over a high heat until the syrup starts to go brown at the edges; do not stir, but you can swirl the pan slightly to make it evenly golden. Continue to cook until the syrup has completely caramelised — it should be slightly smoking, and be the colour of whiskey! This should take about 6–8 minutes altogether. Immediately add the hot water — be aware that it might spit for a second — stir it for a second to mix, then add the halved peaches and the strips of lemon zest. Poach the peaches on a medium heat for 4 or 5 minutes until they have just softened. Take off the heat, allow to cool, remove the lemon zest and add the lemon juice.

Add other fruit as desired; I would add a small punnet of raspberries or blueberries, or a couple of bananas, sliced at an angle; though some-times I use just the peaches. Serve on their own, or with a blob of crème fraîche, or vanilla ice cream. If you have any left over the next morning, have them with some thick natural yoghurt. Yumm. . .

Peach and Strawberry Crumble

Serves 6

The combination of peaches and strawberries is so good, but feel free to replace the strawberries with raspberries or blueberries. This can be made earlier in the day and just popped into the oven to cook when you want it.

300 g (10½ oz) peaches (about 4 peaches), stoned and cut into quarters or eighths
200 g (7 oz) strawberries, halved and quartered
1 tbsp golden caster sugar

for the crumble:
100 g (3½ oz) flour
50 g (2 oz) demerara or golden granulated sugar
50 g (2 oz) butter, chilled and cubed

Preheat oven to 180°C/350°C/gas 4. In a 1-litre (1¾ pt) capacity pie dish (or 6 large ramekins), place the peaches and strawberries. Add the golden caster sugar. For the crumble topping, in a bowl place the flour and demerara or golden granulated sugar. Rub in the butter, but not completely — it should still be nice and coarse. Scatter the crumble over the fruit and refrigerate until you need to cook it. Cook in the preheated oven for 30–40 minutes (or 15–20 for individual dishes) until golden and bubbly. Serve on its own or with a dollop of lightly whipped cream or vanilla ice cream.

NOTE I sometimes add nibbed almonds or chopped hazelnuts, walnuts or pecans to the crumble — just about 25 g (1 oz). Also, sometimes I replace 25 g (1 oz) of the flour with oats.

Banana and Maple Toffee Cake

This is seriously sweet and divine, and fabulous comfort food. It is very quick to make and looks so impressive. You may want to have a dollop of whipped cream on the side!

1 x 25 cm (9¾ in) frying pan, non-stick or not

for the toffee:
50 g (2 oz) butter
25 g (1 oz) brown sugar
50 ml (1¾ fl oz) maple syrup
1 tbsp lemon juice
3 bananas, peeled

for the cake mix:
100 g (3½ oz) butter, softened
50 ml (1¾ fl oz) maple syrup
100 g (3½ oz) brown sugar
1 banana, mashed
3 eggs, beaten
175 g (6 oz) self-raising flour

Preheat the oven to 180°C/350°F/gas 4. To make the toffee, place a 25 cm (9¾ in) frying pan on a medium heat, with the butter, brown sugar and maple syrup. Cook, stirring every now and then for 4 minutes until the toffee has thickened a little. Set aside and sprinkle with lemon juice. To make the cake, cream the butter, add the maple syrup and brown sugar, still beating. Add the mashed banana and eggs, bit by bit, then stir in the flour. Or you can just throw everything into a food processor and whiz briefly till it comes together. Slice the bananas in half horizontally, then in half widthways, and arrange in the pan in a fan shape. Spread the cake mixture over the bananas and place the pan in the preheated oven for 35 minutes or until the cake feels set in the centre. Take it out when cooked, and let it sit for just 5 minutes. Slide a knife around the sides of the pan and turn the cake out onto a plate (it must still be warm to turn out).

NOTE I sometimes find that when I turn this out, quite a bit of toffee remains in the pan. If this happens, place it on the heat, add 1 tbsp water and whisk until it all dissolves, then pour it over the bananas.

See photo between page 112 and 113.

Formal Dinner Party

A few people have asked me what I would cook for a boss, or for someone who would need a little impressing — maybe a mother-in-law (or even scarier, a mother-in-law-to-be!) Personally I think that just very simple food cooked with the minimum fuss is actually impressive enough, but if you want a meal that would show that you are an accomplished cook, you should find something in this chapter. I find the trick is not to take on too much — that will defeat the whole process. It is quite handy to have the starter and the dessert made ahead of time, so you can spend maximum amount of time possible at the table, dazzling everyone with your beauty, wit and intelligence!

Kir Royale

This is a simple and sophisticated classic cocktail. Give your guests a glass of this when they arrive. Buy champagne or a very drinkable sparkling wine. To make a Kir without the Royale, just use white wine.

crème de cassis (blackcurrant liqueur)
chilled champagne or sparkling wine

Pour about ¼ tsp of crème de cassis into the bottom of a champagne glass. Top up with the bubbly and serve. The cassis should just colour the champagne — too much and it will be overpowering in its sweetness.

Potato Soup with Dill and Smoked Salmon

Serves 6

This is a basic potato and onion soup with the addition of dill and smoked salmon, so if you want to try changing it, just leave out the smoked salmon and change the herb to marjoram, tarragon, sage, chives or rosemary, for example. This is so easy for a dinner party — the soup can be made earlier in the day, or even a day before, and just heated up to serve, then sprinkled with the smoked salmon, which just about cooks in the heat of the soup as it goes to the table . . . divine!

50 g (2 oz) butter
400 g (14 oz) potatoes, peeled and chopped
100 g (3½ oz) onions, chopped
a good pinch of salt, and pepper
800 ml (1½ pt) chicken or vegetable stock
125 ml (4½ fl oz) creamy milk (half milk, half cream, or just all milk, if you prefer)
2 tbsp chopped dill
100 g (3½ oz) sliced smoked salmon, cut into little slices, about 2 cm x ½ cm (¾ x ¼ in)

Melt the butter in a large saucepan. Add the potatoes onions, salt and pepper, and stir. Cover with a lid, and sweat on a low heat for 8–10 minutes, stirring every so often, so that the potatoes don't stick and burn. Turn up the heat and add the stock, and boil for about 10 minutes, until the vegetables are completely soft. Purée the soup in a liquidiser, or with a hand whizzer, and add the creamy milk. Thin with more stock, or milk, if you like. Season to taste, and set aside. When you are ready to eat, heat up the soup, add the chopped dill, and ladle into bowls, then sprinkle with the little slices of smoked salmon, and serve.

Salad of Aubergine and Feta, with Crispy Prosciutto

Serves 4

This salad looks lovely on the plate, and tastes great. All the elements of this dish can be prepared in advance, and will just need assembling before you want to sit down.

4 small slices of Parma ham (prosciutto di Parma) or Serrano ham
1 medium aubergine, sliced very thinly
olive oil to brush the aubergine
2 heads of little gem, split in half lengthways, or 12 leaves of cos lettuce
200 g (7 oz) feta cheese, crumbled into 2 cm-ish (¾ in) chunks
8 basil leaves

for the dressing:
2 tbsp olive oil
2 tsp balsamic vinegar
tiny pinch sea salt
freshly ground black pepper

Place the Parma or Serrano ham under a hot grill, and cook for just 1 minute, or until it is crisp. Remove and set aside. To make the dressing, mix the 2 tbsp olive oil and the balsamic vinegar, season with sea salt and pepper to taste, and set aside. Brush the aubergine slices with olive oil, and cook on a very hot grill pan, or frying pan, until golden on both sides. Set aside. Divide the lettuce between the plates — either half heads of baby gem, or 3 whole leaves of cos on each plate. Scatter with the feta cheese and the basil leaves, and divide out the slices of aubergine. Drizzle with the dressing, and place a slice of crisp prosciutto sitting on top. Serve.

NOTE Sometimes I don't grill the Parma ham, but simply serve it as it comes, draped over the salad.

Roast Rack of Spring Lamb with Cumin, Fresh Mint Chutney and Tzatziki

Serves 4–6

A rack of lamb is a gorgeous piece of meat — tender, sweet, and succulent. Of course, if you eat the first of the spring lamb, at Eastertime, the racks will be very small, and each rack, which contains 8 chops, may feed only 2 people, but if you have it a few months later, when the lambs will be slightly older, and bigger, one rack may feed 3 or 4 people. If you don't want to cook racks of lamb, you can, very successfully (especially convenient for 10 or more people), cook a leg of lamb (page 105) and serve it with these sauces — even omitting the sliced potatoes and replacing with Couscous (page 74). Of course, you could serve Redcurrant Jolly (page 108) and/or Fresh Mint Sauce (page 109) instead of the Mint Chutney and Tzatziki here.

2 prepared racks of spring lamb — your butcher will do this for you

salt and freshly ground pepper
2 tbsp freshly ground cumin

Apple and Mint Chutney (see recipe, page 90)
Tzatziki (see recipe, page 91)

to decorate:
sprigs of fresh mint

Remove the thin layer of skin from on top of the fat, and score the fat, not cutting through to the meat. Refrigerate until needed.

Preheat the oven to 220°C/425°F/gas 7.

Sprinkle the fat of the racks of lamb with salt and rub all over with freshly ground pepper and cumin. Roast fat-side upwards for 25–30 minutes, depending on age of lamb and how well cooked you want it to be. Basically, if it is a small spring rack, 25 minutes will be enough, but if you are eating this close to Christmas — when it is at the end of being called 'lamb' and about to be called 'hogget' — for medium, you might want to cook it for 40 minutes.

Meanwhile, make the fresh mint chutney and tzatziki.

When the lamb is cooked, remove to a warm serving dish. Turn off the oven and allow the lamb to rest for 5–10 minutes before carving, to allow the juices to redistribute evenly through the meat. Carve the lamb and serve 2–3 cutlets per person, depending on size. Serve with couscous, apple and mint chutney, and tzatziki.

NOTE To make a Guard of Honour: Prepare (or ask your butcher to prepare) 2 racks of lamb, similar in size. Score the fat in a criss-cross pattern. Hold the two racks facing each other, fat sides pointing out. Adjust them so that the rib bones interlock and cross at the top. Tie with cotton string, around the meat, in a few places to keep them secure. Your butcher might do all this for you!

See photo between page 144 and 145.

Apple and Mint Chutney

Serves 4–6

Great to serve with curries and spicy dishes, this will keep for a couple of days in the fridge. It is even good as a dip for poppadoms before the meal.

1 large cooking apple (e.g. Bramley's seedling), peeled and cored
a large handful of fresh mint leaves
50 g (2 oz) onions
25 g (1 oz) caster sugar
a pinch of cayenne pepper
a pinch of salt

In a food processor (or you can chop everything finely by hand), whiz up all the ingredients, season with a pinch of salt, and add more sugar if it is very tart, or more cayenne if you like it hotter!

See photo between page 144 and 145.

Tzatziki

Serves 10–12

This Greek speciality is a delicious cucumber and yoghurt mixture and can be served as an accompanying salad or as a sauce to serve with grilled fish or meat. Greek yoghurt is thick and creamy. This makes a lot — you can halve the recipe but I love having some of this left over in the fridge to drizzle over baked pototoes, or to fill a warmed split pitta with sliced chicken and tomato.

1 crisp cucumber, halved lengthways, deseeded and diced into ¾ cm (½ in) dice
salt and freshly ground pepper
a dash of wine vinegar or lemon juice
2 cloves of garlic, crushed
1 heaped tbsp freshly chopped mint
450 ml (15¾ fl oz) Greek yoghurt or natural yoghurt (Greek yoghurt is best for this)
2 tbsp cream

Put the cucumber dice in a sieve, sprinkle with salt, and allow to drain for about 30 minutes. Dry the cucumber on kitchen paper. Put it in a bowl and mix together with the garlic, a dash of wine vinegar or lemon juice and the yoghurt and cream. Stir in the mint and taste — it may need a little salt and freshly ground pepper or even a pinch of sugar.

See photo between page 144 and 145.

Roast Fillet of Beef with Red-Wine Glazed Shallots and Horseradish Sauce

Serves 4–6

This is quite a classic dish — a great combination of flavours. If you want to get a bit of prep done in advance, you can seal the beef fillet but set it aside and cook it when you're ready, which means it's great for entertaining. You can make the glazed shallots and horseradish sauce in advance too.

900 g (2 lb) beef fillet
2 tsp freshly ground black pepper (nice if it's a bit coarse)
65 g (2½ oz) butter
450 g (1 lb) shallots, peeled and ends trimmed
200 ml (7 fl oz) beef or chicken stock (I usually use chicken)
1 tsp caster sugar
salt and pepper
2 big sprigs of thyme
250 ml (8¾ fl oz) good red wine

Preheat the oven to 180°C/350°F/gas 4. Season the fillet of beef all over with pepper. Heat a frying pan, till very hot. Add 25 g (1 oz) butter and the whole beef fillet. Turn to sear it all over — the pan must be hot. Place in a roasting tray and set aside if you want, or cook it straightaway in the preheated oven for about 25–30 minutes. Heat a saucepan, and add 25 g (1 oz) butter and the shallots. Cook until golden. Add stock, sugar, salt, pepper and the sprigs of thyme. Boil, uncovered, until it is syrupy. Add the wine and boil again, uncovered, until it has reduced to about half of its original volume. Whisk in the remaining 15 g (½ oz) butter. Taste. When the beef is cooked to your liking, turn off the heat and rest for 10 minutes. Then serve in slices 1 cm (½ in) thick, with the Red-Wine Glazed Shallots, Granny's Roast Potatoes and some Horseradish Sauce. Divine!

Horseradish Sauce

Serves 4–6

It is now quite easy to get hold of fresh horseradish in greengroceries and supermarkets. It's a long root and it lasts for ages. Just peel what you're going to grate and save the rest with the skin on.

3 tbsp grated horseradish
1 tsp white wine vinegar
1 tsp lemon juice
¼ tsp mustard
½ tsp salt
pinch of freshly ground black pepper
1 tsp sugar
225 ml (8 fl oz) softly whipped cream (start with about 125 ml (4½ fl oz) cream)

Mix the horseradish with the wine vinegar, lemon juice, mustard, salt, pepper and sugar. Gently fold in the softly whipped cream. This sauce keeps for a few days.

Granny's Roast Potatoes

Serves 4–6

These are the same potatoes as in my last book. If serving these with roast duck, you could replace some of the olive oil with duck fat.

8 large potatoes, peeled and cut in half
olive oil or beef dripping
salt

Preheat the oven to 200°C/400°F/gas 6. Drop the potatoes into boiling salted water and cook for 10 minutes. Drain off the water and shake the potatoes in the dry saucepan with the lid on — this makes the edges of the potatoes a bit rough. Heat a few tablespoons of olive oil in a roasting tray and toss the potatoes in it, making sure that they're well coated — add more oil if they aren't. Sprinkle with salt and place in the hot oven for 35–55 minutes, spooning the hot oil over them every now and then. Take them out when they are golden brown and crusty.

NOTE If these have to keep warm in the oven for any amount of time, don't cover them. If you do, they'll go soggy.

NOTE Sometimes I toss a few sprigs of thyme, sage or marjoram in, after about 20 minutes of cooking.

See photo between page 48 and 49.

Almond Roulade with Raspberries

This always looks so lovely. Of course, you can replace the raspberries with other fruits if you like — for example, sliced strawberries or peaches. The roulade can be rolled in advance — about 3 or 4 hours at most. The almond sponge can be made days in advance (see below).

1 tbsp sunflower oil
125 g (4½ oz) caster sugar
5 eggs, separated
125 g (4½ oz) ground almonds
50 g (2 oz) flour
a couple of drops of almond essence – beware, this is strong!
300 ml (10½ fl oz) cream, whipped (so about 550 ml (19¾ fl oz) of whipped cream)
225 g (8 oz) raspberries
icing sugar to dust

Preheat the oven to 180°C/350°F/gas 4. Line a 33 x 23 cm (13 x 9 in) swiss-roll tin with tin foil, coming up the sides too. Brush with sunflower oil. Whisk the caster sugar and 5 egg yolks until thick and mousse-like. Fold in the ground almonds, flour and the almond essence. In a clean bowl, whisk the egg whites till stiff, then gently fold into the mixture. Pour into the prepared tin, spread out and bake for 15–18 minutes, until it feels firm in the centre. Remove from the oven and cover with a clean, damp tea towel till cold. (It can be stored like this for a couple of days.) Turn out onto a sheet of tin foil sprinkled generously with icing sugar. Spread with the whipped cream, and scatter with raspberries. Roll up the roulade carefully, transfer onto a plate, dust with icing sugar, and serve.

See photo between page 112 and 113.

Chocolate and Pear Tart

Serves 8

My friend, Dervilla, makes this tart — it is so good and deceptively easy.
It is also very handy as you don't have to bake the pastry blind.

for preparing the tin:
10 g (½ oz) butter, softened
1 tbsp caster sugar

1 x recipe for Sweet Shortcrust Pastry (page 23)

for the custard:
2 eggs
125 ml (4½ fl oz) cream
½ tsp vanilla extract
25 g (1 oz) castor sugar

125 g (4½ oz) dark chocolate, chopped or whizzed up in food processor
3 medium or 4 small ripe pears, peeled, halved, core scooped out with
a teaspoon or melon baller
25 g (1 oz) caster sugar — for sprinkling
1 x 24 cm (9½ in) tart tin with 2 cm (¾ in) high sides

Preheat the oven to 200°C/400°F/gas 6. Butter tin generously and
sprinkle with sugar. Roll the pastry about 3 mm (⅛ in) thick and line the
tin. Place in a freezer for 10 minutes. Make the custard by whisking
the eggs, cream, vanilla and sugar for 3 minutes. Take pastry out of
the freezer. Sprinkle the pastry base with the chopped chocolate,
arrange the pears on top and gently pour over the custard. Sprinkle
with the remaining 25 g (1 oz) caster sugar and bake in the oven,
close to the bottom of the oven, for 10 minutes. Reduce the heat to
170°C/325°F/gas 3 and continue cooking for another 15–20 minutes
until just set in the centre.

Gooseberry Tart

Serves 8

In the months of June and July, when the fresh gooseberries are in season, there is nothing like a gooseberry tart (although frozen gooseberries can be used for this too). The fruit in this tart can be altered, depending on the time of the year (see below for variations).

1 x recipe Sweet Shortcrust Pastry (page 23), made with finely grated rind of 1 small lemon, and baked blind in a 25 x 3 cm (9¾ x 1¼ in) tart tin
3 eggs
100 g (3½ oz) caster sugar
½ tsp vanilla extract
250 ml (8¾ fl oz) cream
450 g (1 lb) fresh, or frozen, gooseberries
100 g (3½ oz) caster sugar and 1 tbsp water

While the pastry is chilling in the fridge, or baking blind, cook the gooseberries: place them in a saucepan with the sugar and water, with the heat very low at first, to dissolve the sugar, Cook the gooseberries until they are soft and have burst — about 4 or 5 minutes. Take off the heat, and let them cool in the juicy syrup that will have formed.

Preheat an oven to 180°C/350°F/gas 4. To make the custard: in a bowl, whisk the eggs with the sugar and the vanilla, then whisk in the cream. Pour the gooseberries into a sieve to get rid of excess juices, then spread the gooseberries over the base of the pastry. Pour the custard into the pastry shell on top of the gooseberries. Place in the preheated oven, and cook for 35–45 minutes, or until the custard in the centre of the tart is set. Let the tart sit for 10 minutes before removing from the tin. To remove from the tin, sit the tin gently on a small bowl, and the sides of the tin should fall onto the work surface; if not, gently ease a small sharp knife around the edge of the tin to un-stick the pastry from the tin. Transfer the tart, still on the base (it can be a bit risky to remove!) to a large plate. When it has cooled a little, dust with a little icing sugar.

To serve, cut the tart into slices, and serve with, if desired, a little whipped cream. Serve ever so slightly warm, or at room temperature.

NOTE Sometimes I slice the gooseberries ½ cm (¼ in) thick, and arrange them on top of the tart instead of cooking them in syrup. Sprinkle generously with granulated sugar and pop under the grill for 2 minutes. This works well if the gooseberries are sweet and ripe — and it looks lovely, too!

See photo betwen page 112 and 113.

Raspberry Tart

Replace the gooseberries with 250 g (9 oz) raspberries, but do not cook in sugar and water — just add in, raw, on their own.

Blueberry Tart

Replace the raspberries with 250 g (9 oz) blueberries.

Caramelised Walnuts with Blue Cheese

Serves 6–8

These caramelised walnuts can be lovely to serve with cheese at the end of a meal. They go particularly well with a good strong blue cheese. They can be made up a week or so in advance — store in an airtight jar.

75 g (3 oz) sugar
75 g (3 oz) walnuts
a nice big wedge of strong blue cheese

Place the sugar and walnuts in a small saucepan on a medium heat, not stirring. Allow the sugar to caramelise slightly at the edges, then swirl the pan to even it out, and allow it to caramelise completely — the nuts will toast at the same time. Carefully pour out of the saucepan onto parchment paper, or non-stick paper (it will stick to plain greaseproof). Allow to cool and harden, then break up slightly to separate the nuts. Serve on the side of the plate with cheese.

NOTE Take the cheese out of the fridge at least 20 minutes before serving so that it's not cold.

Sunday Lunch

Sunday lunch, for me, means good old-fashioned food — a delicious roast followed by some little pavlovas with cream and fruit, or rhubarb pudding. It is the kind of food that sets you and yours up for the rest of the day, with maybe some leftovers to be devoured for supper later on.

Cannellini Bean and Chicken Soup with Basil

Serves 4–6

This is a very quick soup to make. I would use marjoram, or even coriander if I didn't have basil, and I sometimes leave out the chicken!

2 tbsp olive oil
1 medium onion (about 125 g (4½ oz)) finely chopped
1 clove of crushed or grated garlic
1 x 400g (14 oz) tin of cannellini beans, or haricot beans, drained
600 ml (1 pt) chicken or vegetable stock, heated up in a separate saucepan
2 small chicken breasts, skinned and finely sliced
salt and black pepper
10 large basil leaves

In a saucepan, place the olive oil, chopped onion and the garlic. Season with salt and pepper, and cook on a gentle heat, with the lid on, for about 10 minutes, until the onion is soft. Add the beans and hot stock, and bring to the boil. Simmer for 5 minutes, add more stock if desired, then add the chicken. Simmer for 3 minutes, or until the chicken is cooked, add the basil, then season to taste, and serve.

NOTE If you want to make this in advance, it's best to cook the chicken just before you want to serve it — so proceed up to the point of adding the chicken, and set aside.

Broad Beans with Lemon Zest and Soft Goat's Cheese

Serves 4–6

When I cooked on *Saturday Kitchen* with Antony Worrall Thompson, he made something like this, and it is excellent — very healthy and quick to rustle up.

400 g (14 oz) raw broad beans, out of the pod — no need to peel off the skin
1½ tbsp olive oil
1 tsp finely grated lemon zest
1 tbsp lemon juice
sea salt and freshly ground black pepper
125 g (4½ oz) soft goat's cheese (I love the Irish Ardsallagh Goat's Cheese), or feta works well too, or pecorino

Place the broad beans in a bowl. Add the olive oil, lemon zest and lemon juice; season to taste. Divide out onto plates, and crumble the cheese over the top.

Chicken Baked with Mushrooms and Marjoram

Serves 6

2–3 tbsp olive oil
1 chicken, about 1.5–2.25 kg (3¼–5 lb), jointed and skinned (see below),
or about 6 large chicken breasts
200 ml (7 fl oz) white wine (optional)
200 ml (7 fl oz) chicken stock
2 sprigs of marjoram, or tarragon would be delicious instead
a dash of olive oil
500 g (17½ oz) mushrooms
250 ml (9 fl oz) cream
about 25 g (1 oz) roux (recipe below)
2 tbsp chopped marjoram, or tarragon

Preheat an oven to 190°C/375°F/gas 5. Cut the chicken into portions by first of all removing the legs. Cut the drumsticks away from the thighs and set aside. Remove the wish bone at the neck end, then cut one-third of each breast off with each wing — I normally remove the small wing tip. Then remove each remaining chicken breast. That's your chicken jointed.

Heat up a large sauté pan or saucepan — it shouldn't be too deep, if possible. When the pan is nice and hot, add 2–3 tbsp olive oil and start to brown the pieces of chicken on both sides (about 5 minutes on either side). Add the wine, stock, and the 2 whole sprigs of herbs, bring up to the boil, put a lid on the pan and place in the preheated oven for 30 minutes or until the chicken is cooked. While the chicken is cooking, slice, then sauté, the mushrooms in a tiny dash of olive oil till golden brown. When the chicken is cooked, discard the sprigs of marjoram, and remove the meat and cover it to retain its juices. With the lid off, boil down the stock till it has strengthened in flavour; it should be about 250 ml (9 fl oz) by now. Add the cream, boil for a minute or two, and add the lemon juice. While it is still on a low boil, whisk in the roux (recipe below) until it thickens a little. If it is too thick, just add a little stock to thin it out — it shouldn't be too thick. Add the sautéed mushrooms and chopped herbs, and season to taste. Serve with Pilaff Rice (page 191), Buttered Leeks (page 108) and a big green salad.

NOTE Of course you could leave the cream out of this — it will be very different, but lovely too.

Roux

This is a basic sauce thickener, so it is very handy to have a little of it in the fridge for sauces like the chicken (above) or for gravy. It is just equal quantities of butter and flour, so you could make this with 50 g (2 oz) of each or 1 kg (2¼ lb) of each. It keeps for weeks in the fridge; it will harden but it's perfect.

Melt the butter. Add the flour and stir over a medium heat for 2 minutes. Remove from the heat and use hot or cold.

Roast Leg of Lamb with Sliced Potatoes

Serves 6–8

This method of cooking the potatoes under, and around, the lamb gives the potatoes the most incredible flavour. I love this with a really good mint sauce (or jelly), or some redcurrant jelly, or the Fresh Mint Chutney and the Tzatziki on pages 90 & 91.

1.5–2 kg (3¼–4½ lb) leg or shoulder of lamb
1 tbsp olive oil
1½ tsp cracked black pepper (it's nice if it's still a little coarse)
1 generous tbsp chopped rosemary
1 big pinch of sea salt, such as Maldon, and pepper
1.5–2 kg potatoes (3¼–4½ lb) (about 12–16 big ones), peeled and sliced about ½ cm (¼ in) thick
6–10 cloves of garlic, peeled, left whole

Preheat an oven to 230°C/450°F/gas 8. With a skewer or tip of a knife, prick the skin of the lamb all over about 20–30 times. Mix together the olive oil, pepper and rosemary, and spread all over the lamb, pushing it into the holes. Then sprinkle over the sea salt. Place it in a roasting tray and put it into the preheated oven. Cook for 20 minutes, then turn the heat down to 180°C/350°F/gas 4, and take out the roasting tray. Lift the lamb off the tray and cover the bottom of the tray with the sliced potatoes and the garlic. Season with salt and pepper, and place the lamb on top. Put it back into the oven and cook for about another 70 minutes, I allow 20 minutes per 500 g (17½ oz) at this heat. Turn the potatoes once in the fat while they're cooking. If you like, you can turn the heat back up to 230°C/450°F/gas 8 for the last 15 minutes if the skin has not crisped up enough, though this is normally not necessary. When the lamb is cooked, take it out and place it on something else, covered with tin foil — somewhere warm if possible — and allow to rest for at least 10 minutes. (This tenderises the meat.) Continue cooking the potatoes while the lamb is resting. Once the potatoes are cooked, serve, with all the gravy-type juices in the pan.

Garlic Layered Potatoes

Serves 5–6

My sister, Simone, makes the very best Garlic Layered Potatoes. She says that the key is not to be worried — and, in turn, mean — with the cream. She also always makes sure to serve a lovely light starter (like a salad), if having one before this, and something very fresh to follow, such as mangoes and bananas with lime and honey. This is a perfect accompaniment to roast meat — or, indeed, as a meal in itself, with the addition of anchovies, spinach and olives, smoked salmon, or even chorizo sausage (see below).

25 g (1 oz) soft butter
800 g (1¾ lb) peeled potatoes (I weigh these when peeled), sliced ½ cm (¼ in) thick
salt and pepper
2 small pinches of freshly ground nutmeg (use a very fine grater for this)
2 large cloves of chopped garlic
250 ml (8¾ fl oz) cream
40 g (1½ oz) finely grated parmesan cheese

Preheat the oven to 180°C/350°F/gas 4. Using about 1 tsp butter, grease an ovenproof gratin dish — I use a 1-litre (1¾ pt) pie dish for this quantity. Divide the potatoes in three, and place one-third of the sliced potatoes on the base of the dish. Season with a pinch of salt, pepper, grated/ ground nutmeg, and half of the chopped garlic, then dot with butter. Add another layer of potatoes, and season it in the same way, using the remainder of the garlic. Then add a third layer of potatoes, seasoning them again, and pour over the cream (it should come just over halfway up the sides of the dish). Scatter with the finely grated parmesan, or something similar (cheddar is just too creamy for this). Cover with tin foil and place in the oven for 1¼ to 1½ hours, taking off the tin foil after 30 minutes. The potatoes should be soft and the top should be golden, with the cream bubbling up the sides of the dish.

NOTE If this needs to sit and keep warm in the oven for half an hour or so, cover it to prevent it from drying out.

Layered Potatoes with Anchovies

I sometimes add chopped anchovies in between the layers of potatoes, omitting the nutmeg. Use 1 x 55 g (2 oz) tin (about 12 fillets), or less, if you prefer.

Layered Potatoes with Spinach and Olives

In between each layer of potatoes, not omitting the nutmeg, add 1 tbsp (about 15 g (½ oz)) chopped, stoned black olives (or the same of tapenade/olive paste), and 1 large handful (about 25 g (1 oz)) spinach leaves (de-stalk and chop if the leaves are large).

Layered Potatoes with Smoked Salmon

In between each layer of potatoes, scatter 50 g (2 oz) chopped smoked salmon. I would omit the grated parmesan for this.

Layered Potatoes with Chorizo

In between each layer of potatoes, scatter 25 g (1 oz) chopped, or sliced, chorizo.

Buttered Leeks

Serves 4–6

6 medium leeks (about 1 kg), dark green tops removed
25 g (1 oz) butter
scant 2 tbsp water
salt and pepper

Wash the leeks well and remove the root part at the bottom. Cut into round slices about 8–10 mm (¼–½ in) thick. Melt the butter in a saucepan with the water. Add the leeks and toss gently. Season with a pinch of salt and pepper. Reduce the heat to very low, place the lid on the pan, and cook for about 10–20 minutes until just cooked. Do not overcook them; they should not lose their fresh green colour.

Redcurrant Jelly

Makes 1 big jar

If you want to make your own redcurrant jelly, it is actually very quick and easy, keeps for months, and, of course, you can use frozen redcurrants.

500 g (17½ oz) redcurrants, de-stalked
500 g (17½ oz) sugar

Place the redcurrants and sugar in a big saucepan and stir over a medium heat until the sugar dissolves and the mixture comes to the boil. Turn up the heat and boil for 6 minutes, stirring every now and then to prevent it from sticking to the bottom of the pan. Spoon off any froth that has floated to the top, and pour the mixture into a sieve (not aluminium). Allow it to drip through — don't push it — otherwise it will be a cloudy jelly. If you want to keep this for a while, pour the jelly into clean, sterilised jam jars straightaway. It will be ready to eat once it has cooled and set a little, or you could keep it in the fridge for whenever you want it.

Fresh Mint Sauce

Serves 6

This is so good if you have lots of mint. It is best made on the day you want to eat it.

3 tbsp chopped mint
1 good tbsp sugar
50 ml (2 fl oz) boiling water (straight out of the kettle)
1 tbsp lemon juice or white wine vinegar

Put the mint and sugar into a bowl. Add the boiling water, stir to dissolve the sugar, and then add the lemon juice or vinegar. Let it sit for 10 minutes before serving.

Polenta, Almond and Lemon Cake

Serves 8–10

This recipe was inspired by the cake of the same name from *The River Café Cookbook*. It is wonderful served with a little dollop of Greek yoghurt and some fresh berries on the side, or the Compote of Berries (page 112), or on its own with a cup of coffee! It is so moist, it keeps for ages.

butter and 1 dessertspoon flour or polenta for tin
225 g (8 oz) soft butter
225 g (8 oz) caster sugar
3 eggs, beaten
finely grated zest and juice of 1 lemon
a few drops of almond essence — optional
200 g (7 oz) ground almonds
125 g (4½ oz) medium polenta (maize meal). I get this in a health-food shop
1 tsp baking powder

to serve:
a little icing sugar to dust the top

Preheat the oven to 170°C/325°F/gas 3. Place a disc of greaseproof paper in the bottom of a 20 cm (8 in) cake tin, which must be 5 cm (2 in) high. Butter the sides of the tin and dust with 1 dessertspoon of flour, or polenta. Cream the butter, add the sugar and mix well. Beat in the eggs, one at a time, then add the lemon zest and juice, and the almond essence, if using. Fold in the ground almonds, polenta, and the baking powder. Put the cake mixture into the prepared tin, and cook in the preheated oven for 58–68 minutes or until a skewer inserted into the centre of the cake comes out clean. Sometimes, depending on the oven, I quickly place a piece of tin foil on top of the cake after 45 minutes, to prevent it from getting too brown. Take it out of the oven when it is cooked, and let it cool in the tin for about 10 minutes before removing it. To serve, dust it with a little icing sugar.

Apple Pudding

Serves 6–8

This is wonderful comfort food — great with a little whipped cream or some vanilla ice cream on the side. I like to serve this slightly warm, so warm it up if it has not just come out of the oven.

450 g (1 lb) cooking apples, peeled, core removed, and chopped
roughly, weighed afterwards
125 g (4½ oz) sugar
1 tbsp water
125 g (4½ oz) soft butter
125 g (4½ oz) caster sugar
2 eggs, beaten
½ tsp vanilla extract
125 g (4½ oz) self-raising flour

25 g (1 oz) caster sugar, for sprinkling

Preheat the oven to 180°C/350°F/gas 4. Place the apples, sugar and water in a small saucepan on a low heat. With the lid on, cook for about 10 minutes, stirring every now and then, until the apples are soft. Pour into a 1-litre (1¾ pt) shallow pie dish, or into 8 individual ramekins.

In a bowl, beat the butter. Add the sugar and beat again, then add the eggs and the vanilla, gradually, still beating, then fold in the flour to combine. Spread this over the apple, sprinkle with sugar and cook in the preheated oven for 40–50 minutes until the centre of the sponge feels firm, or a skewer inserted into the centre comes out clean.

NOTE This is also lovely with a handful of fresh or frozen blackberries added to the apples in the saucepan.

Rhubarb Pudding

Serves 6–8

This is gorgeous served in late spring/summer when the rhubarb is in season, or made with frozen rhubarb throughout the year.

As for Apple Pudding above, but instead of the cooking apple, use 450 g (1 lb) of sliced (1 cm (½ in) thick) fresh or frozen rhubarb.

Compote of Berries

Serves 4–6, or if serving with the cake, this would serve 8–10

These berries are lovely served with the Polenta, Almond and Lemon Cake (page 110); or of course just on their own, with some whipped cream or crème fraîche on the side. You can use fresh or frozen fruit for this — no need to thaw. If you don't have any fruit in your freezer, look in the freezer department in your supermarket for bags of mixed berries.

400 g (14 oz) mixed berries — like raspberries, strawberries, blackberries, blackcurrants, redcurrants
100 g (3½ oz) sugar
100 ml (3½ fl oz) water
juice of ½–1 lemon

Place the mixed fruit in a bowl. In a small saucepan, put the sugar and water, and stir over a low heat for a minute until the sugar dissolves, then turn up the heat and boil the syrup for a minute. Pour over the fresh or frozen fruit. Allow to cool before adding the lemon juice to taste. This is best made at least half an hour in advance.

Roasted Tomato and Basil Soup, Basil Pesto and Chilli Croutons
(page 116)

Tomatoes for Roasted Tomato and Basil Soup (page 116)

Irish Hot Chocolate with Chocolate and Almond Biscotti (pages 159 & 146)

Little Pistachio Pavlovas with Poached Apricots and Cardamom
(pages 113 & 114)

Strawberry and Honey Mascarpone Tart (page 69)

Gooseberry Tart (page 97)

Banana and Maple Toffee Cake (page 82)

Almond Roulade with Raspberries (page 95)

Little Pistachio Pavlovas

Makes 6 individual pavlovas

I love the combination of the pistachios with the cardamom-scented apricots, and the light, almost chewy texture, of the pavlovas.

100 g (3½ oz) shelled pistachios
4 egg whites or 100 ml (3½ fl oz) egg whites from the fridge
200 g (7 oz) caster sugar
1 tsp white wine vinegar
2 tsp cornflour
½ tsp vanilla extract

to serve:
200 ml (7 fl oz) whipped cream
Poached Apricots with Cardamom (page 114)

Preheat oven to 140°C/275°F/gas 1. Line a baking tray with parchment paper. With an electric beater, whisk the egg whites until they form soft peaks, then gradually add the sugar and continue whisking until the mixture is stiff and glossy. Stop whisking and add all but 2 tsp of the chopped nuts, together with the vinegar, cornflour and vanilla, and fold in really gently. Using two spoons, place 6 big dollops of meringue on the paper and, with a spoon, make slight hollows in the centres. Sprinkle with the remaining nuts and bake for 30 minutes, until crisp on the outside. Then turn the oven off and leave to sit for another half an hour in the oven.

When these are cool, and you want to serve them, place one pavlova on each plate, add a dollop of cream, then spoon over a few poached apricots with cardamom. If you like, scatter with some more nuts.

NOTE I sometimes use toasted almonds or hazelnuts instead of the pistachios (rub the skin off the hazelnuts after toasting them) or, of course, this is also a lovely recipe without any nuts.

Poached Apricots with Cardamom

Serve these with Pistachio Pavlovas above.

450 g (1 lb) fresh apricots or 225 g (8 oz) dried apricots
12 green cardamom pods
1 l (1¾ pt) water
300 g (10½ oz) sugar (or just 175 g (6 oz) if using dried apricots)
2 tbsp lemon juice

If you are using dried apricots, soak them in boiling water for 10 minutes. Bash the cardamom pods slightly and put them into a saucepan with the water and sugar. Bring to the boil, add the apricots and simmer till tender — this takes about 20 minutes. Cool, add the lemon juice, and serve with a dollop of crème fraîche or with the pistachio meringues.

See photo between page 112 and 113.

Big Family Lunch

This is the kind of meal where you will have lots of family and close friends over to the house — maybe a birthday or a big wedding anniversary, or a christening. You want food that is just as easy to make for 30 people as it is for 6; food that children and grown-ups alike will enjoy; and food that can all be prepared in advance.

Roasted Tomato and Basil Soup

Serves 4–6

This soup is fantastic made in summer with really good, ripe tomatoes, and it freezes well too. Instead of basil, you could use mint, coriander or tarragon.

1.1 kg (2½ lb) ripe tomatoes (about 10–12 large tomatoes)
3 cloves of garlic, peeled
1 sprig of basil
3 tbsp olive oil
salt, pepper and sugar
150 g (5 oz) onion, chopped
25 g (1 oz) butter or 2 tbsp olive oil
425 ml (¾ pt) chicken or vegetable stock
2 tbsp chopped basil
croutons — optional (See recipe for Caesar Salad page 60)
basil pesto — optional

Preheat the oven to 240°C/475°F/gas 9. Cut the tomatoes into quarters, then in half again, removing the little core. Spread them out in a large roasting tray. Add the peeled garlic cloves and the whole sprig of basil, drizzle over the olive oil, and season generously with salt, pepper and sugar. Place the tray in the hot oven and roast for 30–40 minutes, until the tomatoes are soft and a little browned.

Meanwhile, sweat the onions in the butter or olive oil until very soft and almost golden. Add the tomatoes, garlic and all the juices — you can discard the basil sprig now. Add the stock. Bring this to the boil and simmer for 5 minutes, seasoning more if it needs it. Liquidise the soup. Chop or finely slice the basil and add to the soup. Add more stock if you think it needs it, or you could even add a dash of cream. Reheat the soup and serve.

Sprinkle each bowl of soup with croutons if you are using them, or just serve with some lovely bread, toasted then drizzled with olive oil.

NOTE This is also good with a little basil pesto drizzled on at the end.

See photo between page 112 and 113.

Cauliflower and Cheddar Cheese Soup

Serves 6

We make a soup like this at the cookery school, and it is so yummy — a great wintertime soup.

for the cheese sauce:
600 ml (1 pt) milk
½ carrot
½ onion
sprig of thyme and parsley
15 g (½ oz) butter
15 g (½ oz) (1 tbsp) flour
110 g (4 oz) grated good cheddar cheese
½ tsp Dijon mustard
salt and pepper

1 big head of cauliflower (about 850 g (1¾ lb), outer green leaves, and big stalk removed
400 ml (14 fl oz) chicken or vegetable stock
1 tbsp chopped parsley

To make the cheese sauce, place the milk, vegetables and herbs in a saucepan, bring up to a simmer, and simmer for 2 or 3 minutes, careful not to over-boil. Turn off the heat, and leave to infuse for a few minutes — to get plenty of flavour — then drain, and discard the carrot, onion and herbs. If you are in a rush, you can leave out the vegetables and herbs and the simmering. Either way, in another saucepan, melt the butter, add the flour, and stir over a medium heat for 2 minutes, then gradually add the milk, on the heat, whisking to prevent lumps from forming. Boil for 2 minutes until the sauce has thickened. Take off the heat, and add the grated cheese, and the mustard and salt and pepper to taste. This is your cheese sauce.

Chop up the cauliflower. Place in a saucepan, cover with the stock, and cook for about 5 minutes, or until the cauliflower is just soft. Add the cheese sauce, and liquidise. Season to taste, adding more stock if it is too thick. Add the chopped parsley and serve.

Beef Bourguignon

Serves 6

Another classic, this is a slightly simplified version. For entertaining of any kind, it is great as it can be made the previous day. I love to eat this with Garlic Layered Potatoes (page 106) or Nutmeg Mash (page 120).

2 tbsp olive oil
200 g (7 oz) streaky bacon, cut into 1 cm (½ in) cubes
18 baby onions or shallots, peeled
1.5 kg (3¼ lb) stewing beef, cut into 4 cm (1½ in) cubes
pepper
40 g (1½ oz) flour
400 ml (14 fl oz) red wine
4 cloves of finely chopped garlic
1 bay leaf
1 sprig thyme
2 stalks parsley
small piece of orange zest
450 ml (¾ pt) beef or chicken stock
18 small button mushrooms, tossed in a hot pan with a small knob of butter (about 25 g (1 oz)), till golden

Preheat the oven to 160°C/325°F/gas 3. In a casserole or a large saucepan, heat 1 tbsp olive oil and brown the bacon. Remove and set aside, leaving any fat in the saucepan. Add the onions and cook those, stirring on a high heat till golden, then take out and add to the bacon. Pop the beef into the hot pan in batches, and cook till brown. Season with pepper. Put all the beef back into the pan and scatter in the flour, stirring the meat all the time. Pour in the wine and garlic. Stir again and add the bay, thyme, parsley and orange zest (I sometimes tie these up with string so that I can pull them out easily later). Add the bacon and onions again, and enough stock to come about three-quarters of the way up the ingredients in the pot. Bring up to the boil, put the lid on, and place in a preheated oven for 2½ hours until almost tender. Add the mushrooms and continue to cook the stew for another 30–40 minutes or until the beef is tender. Remove the orange zest and herbs, correct the seasoning, and serve.

NOTE If making this a day or two in advance, I would add the mushrooms and finish cooking it on the day it is to be eaten, for the best results.

Nutmeg Mash

Serves 6

1 kg (2¼ lb) floury potatoes
50 g (2 oz) butter
200 ml (7 fl oz) boiling milk
½ tsp grated/ground nutmeg
salt and pepper

I find this the best way to cook good, fluffy, floury potatoes. Clean the potatoes and put them in a saucepan of cold water with a good pinch of salt. Bring the water up to the boil and cook for 10 minutes. Pour all but 4 cm (1½ in) of the water out and continue to cook the potatoes on a very low heat. Don't be tempted to stick a knife into them — the skins will break and they'll just break up and get soggy if you do. About 20 minutes later, when you think they might be ready, test them with a skewer; if they're soft, take them off the heat.

Peel the potatoes while they're still hot and mash them straightaway. Add the butter, but don't add any milk till it is smooth. Then add the boiling milk. You might need more, depending on the potatoes. Add salt, pepper and nutmeg. If you want to make this in advance, add a little extra milk to prevent it from drying out. It will keep well, covered with tin foil, a plate or a lid, in a warm oven.

Spinach and Ricotta Lasagne

Serves 8–10

This is the perfect, prepare-in-advance dish. You can even make it the previous day, if you like, and bake it when you are ready to serve. It would also freeze for a few weeks — thaw overnight in the fridge. Serve with a big green salad.

450 g (1 lb) dried sheets (or fresh) lasagne
1 kg (2¼ lb) spinach leaves, washed
1 tbsp water
450 g (1 lb) ricotta (2 x 225g (8 oz) tubs)
50 g (2 oz) melted butter
¼–½ tsp ground nutmeg

for the béchamel sauce:
150 g (5 oz) butter
150 g (5 oz) flour
1.5 l (2½ pt) milk
salt and pepper
¼–½ tsp ground nutmeg

100 g (3½ oz) grated parmesan cheese

You will need a lasagne dish 30 x 25 cm (12 x 10 in) or 2 smaller 20 x 25 cm (8 x 10 in) dishes

Preheat the oven to 180°C/350°F/gas 4. Heat up a large saucepan of boiling, salted water and blanch the lasagne sheets in batches, 3 or 4 at a time, for 4 minutes, until half cooked. Take out and place on clean tea towels or greaseproof paper, in a single layer.

To make the béchamel sauce, melt the butter in a large saucepan (same one you used for blanching the pasta), whisk in the flour and stir on the heat for 2 minutes. Remove from the heat and gradually add the milk, whisking all the time. Place back on the heat and bring to the boil to thicken. Add salt, pepper and nutmeg to taste.

Place the spinach in a saucepan. Add 1 tablespoon of water and cook on a low heat, stirring regularly for about 4 minutes, until the spinach has softened. Drain completely (squeeze it in kitchen paper to remove excess moisture), and chop roughly. Mix in a bowl, with the crumbled ricotta cheese and the melted butter. Add nutmeg, and season to taste.

Spread a thin layer of béchamel sauce on the base of the lasagne dish. Cover with a layer of barely overlapping sheets of pasta. Spread one-third of the spinach and ricotta mixture over the pasta, spread one-third of the béchamel sauce over the spinach and ricotta, and sprinkle with a third of the parmesan cheese. Repeat for two more layers, ending with grated parmesan on top. When you want to serve this, place in preheated oven for 25 minutes or till golden and bubbly.

NOTE I sometimes mix 100 g (3½ oz) of toasted pine nuts in with the spinach and ricotta mix.

Hazelnut Toffee Meringues with Butterscotch Sauce and Bananas

Makes 6, serves 6

for the meringues:

2 egg whites or 50 ml/50 g (2 fl oz/2 oz) egg whites from the fridge (see note on page 125)
100 g (3½ oz) soft brown sugar or muscovado
50 g (2 oz) roughly chopped hazelnuts (optional)

for the Butterscotch Sauce:

This recipe makes plenty — you might even have some left over — but it keeps in the fridge for weeks and is divine drizzled, warm, over vanilla ice cream.

50 g (2 oz) butter
75 g (3 oz) soft brown sugar or muscovado
50 g (2 oz) sugar, caster or granulated
125 g (4½ oz) golden syrup
100 ml (3½ fl oz) cream
¼ tsp vanilla essence

to serve:
200 ml (7 fl oz) whipped cream
2–3 bananas

Line a baking tray with parchment paper. Preheat the oven to 150°C/300°F/gas 2. To make meringues, in a clean, dry bowl, whisk the egg whites and brown sugar for about 5 minutes until they are a pale beige colour and hold a stiff peak. Using a tablespoon, place 6 dollops of meringue on the baking tray lined with parchment paper. Spread each one out to a circle about 8 or 10 cm (3–4 in) in diameter, and make a slight hollow in the centre. Scatter the meringues with the hazelnuts (if you are using them). Place in the preheated oven and cook for 45 minutes or until they feel crisp on the outside and come away from the paper. Turn off the oven and allow the meringues to cool down gradually, if possible.

Meanwhile, make the butterscotch sauce. Place all the ingredients in a small saucepan. Melt slowly, stirring, then simmer for about 2 or 3 minutes until smooth. Set aside.

To serve, place one cooled meringue on each plate. Spoon a big dollop of whipped cream on top. Add some slices of banana, and drizzle with some butterscotch sauce.

Strawberry Ice Cream

Serves 12 people

This ice cream is really light and gorgeous — perfect for a summer party. Of course, you could halve the recipe here, but I love having some of this in the freezer to dip into. My children love this scooped on a cone. No ice-cream machine needed here.

250 g (9 oz) fresh strawberries (you could use frozen strawberries too)
juice of 1 lemon
250 g (9 oz) caster sugar
200 ml (7 fl oz) water
4 large egg whites or 100 g (4 oz) egg whites
a pinch of cream of tartar (Bextartar)
300 ml (10½ fl oz) cream, whipped (this should come to about 500 ml (17½ fl oz) whipped cream)

Purée the strawberries with the lemon juice (you can use a liquidiser or food processor to do this, or you could mash them with a fork, but be careful not to leave them too rough as they can get a bit icy!) Push the purée through a sieve to remove the seeds. Place the sugar and water in a saucepan, and heat slowly, stirring to dissolve the sugar. Boil fiercely for 5 minutes, until it thickens and the last drops off a spoon dipped into it form a kind of thread. Meanwhile, using an electric whisk, whisk the egg whites with the cream of tartar until stiff. Still whisking, gradually pour in the hot syrup in a thin stream, and continue to whisk until the mixture is cool, glossy, and stiff (about 4 or 5 minutes). Fold in the strawberry purée and the whipped cream, though not completely — I quite like to leave this slightly marbled. Freeze overnight. This ice cream can be scooped straight from the freezer.

NOTE 1 egg white is 25 ml (1 fl oz), or 25 g (1 oz) on the scales, so if you forget how many you have in the fridge, just measure them — 100 ml (4 fl oz) or 100 g (4 oz) for this recipe. Egg whites last for weeks in the fridge — but don't cover them completely — and they also freeze well in a bag or tub; thaw them out overnight in the fridge before use.

Rhubarb Ice Cream

Serves 12 people

Like the Strawberry Ice Cream, this is the most lovely, light ice cream. It is also delicious with some ginger added (see below).

250 g (9 oz) rhubarb, finely sliced
50 g (2 oz) sugar
1 tbsp water

juice of ½ lemon
250 g (9 oz) caster sugar
200 ml (7 fl oz) water
5 large egg whites (see note above)
a pinch of cream of tartar (Bextartar)
300 ml (10½ fl oz) cream, whipped (this should come to about 500 ml (17½ fl oz) whipped cream)

Place the rhubarb, 50 g (2 oz) sugar and water in a small saucepan on a low heat, and stir to dissolve the sugar. Bring up to the boil and cook for a few minutes until the rhubarb has softened to a pulp. Pour it out onto a plate and allow it to cool, then add the lemon juice. Place the 250 g (9 oz) sugar and water in a saucepan, and heat slowly, stirring to dissolve the sugar. Boil fiercely for 5 minutes, until it thickens and the last drops off a spoon dipped into it form a kind of thread. Meanwhile, using an electric whisk, whisk the egg whites with the cream of tartar until stiff. Still whisking, gradually pour in the hot syrup in a thin stream, and continue to whisk until the mixture is cool, glossy, and stiff (about 4 or 5 minutes). Fold in the rhubarb purée and the whipped cream, though not completely — I quite like to leave this slightly marbled. Freeze overnight. This ice cream can be scooped straight from the freezer.

Rhubarb and Ginger Ice Cream

Make as above, but add 2 tsp finely grated ginger to the rhubarb purée with the lemon juice, when it is cool.

Girls' Night In

I love a good girls' night in, even if I don't do it nearly often enough. For this kind of evening, I love a few really yummy tasty dishes that don't require huge amounts of work, but that everyone will enjoy grazing over for hours, while catching up on the latest news over a couple of cocktails.

A Whole Lot of Rosé — Rosé Cocktail

Serves 2

I promised Isaac that I would call this cocktail by this name after some AC/DC song back in the '80s! This is a great summertime drink for sipping on a balmy evening. Serve it nicely chilled. For a non-alcoholic version, replace the rosé with sparkling water.

1 peach or nectarine, stone cut out, and quartered
2 tsp caster sugar
juice of ½ lime or 1 tbsp lime juice
150 ml (5 fl oz) rosé wine — chilled

Whiz up the peach, sugar and lime juice. Add the rosé and pour into two of your favourite wine glasses. Enjoy!

Grenadine Goddess

Serves 2, if in a highball glass, or 4 in martini glasses

A great non-alcoholic cocktail that looks so pretty too.

50 ml (2 fl oz) grenadine (a sweet syrup made mainly from pomegranates)
25 ml (1 fl oz) lime juice (the juice of about ½ lime)
250 ml (8¾ fl oz) slightly crushed ice (bashed up in a bag with a rolling pin)
350 ml (12¼ fl oz) soda water, or sparkling water
2 lime wedges, to decorate

Mix the grenadine and lime juice, and divide into glasses. Add the ice, top up with soda water, and stir. Place a wedge of lime on the side of each glass, and serve.

NOTE To make this a cocktail with alcohol, add 25–50 ml (1–2 fl oz) vodka to each glass.

Chilli and Garlic Pitta Crisps

Serves 4–6

Nice to have on the side at a barbecue, or as an accompaniment to a spicy meal, or just to dip into yummy things, to have with drinks. . .

200 g (7 oz) pitta bread (4 round ones), cut into wedges
50 ml (2 fl oz) olive oil
2 cloves of garlic, grated or crushed
½ red chilli, deseeded and chopped
sea salt

Preheat an oven to 200°C/400°F/gas 6. Cut the pitta bread and place in a bowl. In another bowl, mix the olive oil, garlic and chilli. Pour over the pitta and toss. Place with the little bits of chilli and garlic on a baking tray in a single layer. Sprinkle with sea salt, then cook in the oven for 7–8 minutes, or until golden brown.

Chicken Liver Crostini

Serves about 8–12 as part of an antipasto plate

I love chicken liver pâté, This one is quite strong and gutsy in flavour.
If you like it more rich and creamy, add another 75 g (3 oz) butter.

150 g (5 oz) chicken livers, with any membrane or fatty bits removed
1 tbsp olive oil
2 tbsp marsala, port, or brandy
1 clove of crushed or grated garlic
1 tsp chopped sage, or thyme, or slightly less of rosemary
75 g (3 oz) butter

Fry the livers in the olive oil over a low to medium heat till cooked
through. While they are cooking, measure the alcohol into a small bowl.
When the livers are cooked, transfer to a food processor, and whiz up
till fine. Put the pan back on the heat — do NOT wash it first! Add the
alcohol, garlic and chopped herbs. BE VERY CAREFUL — IF THE PAN
IS VERY HOT, IT WILL FLAME, and it is perfect if it does, but you need
to stand back, just for 10 seconds or so. Hold the bottle of alcohol at
a distance from the pan. Then pour the flamed brandy into the food
processor, scraping out all the nice bits from the pan in on top of the
livers. Whiz again, and leave to cool before you add the butter —
otherwise the butter will melt, and you will need to chill it and whiz it
again. When it has cooled, add the butter, while whizzing, until it is
smooth. Season to taste. Serve a slightly spread-out spoonful of this
on crostini, or good toast, and eat! These will sit happily on the crostini
or toast for at least 20 minutes.

NOTE If the thought of the flaming of the alcohol is making you feel
slightly ill at ease, just boil the alcohol in a high-sided saucepan with the
garlic and herbs for 2 minutes. This will still burn the alcohol off but is
not so dramatic.

NOTE Crostini with Parma Ham, Goat's Cheese and Onion Jam (page
42) are also great on an antipasto plate.

Antipasto

Antipasto is Italian for 'before the meal', so refers to foods served as appetisers before the meal begins; but many people, myself included, like to eat a lovely big antipasto plate as a meal in itself. Other versions of this are the Spanish *tapas*, French *hors d'oeuvres*, Scandinavian *smorgassbord*, Russian *zakuski*, or *mezze*, which originated in Persia, but is now seen in Turkey, Greece, and through North Africa to Morocco.

For an antipasto plate, many, if not all, of the elements can be bought ready to serve, so it is fabulous food for entertaining. I love the variety of it, with lots of different flavours, colours, and textures.

Serve it with good crusty white bread, and a bowl of your best olive oil to dip the bread into. On an antipasto plate, I like to put some, or all, of the following. I have given some recipes for various dishes here, but sometimes, if time is of the essence, I would pick up all of the dishes at my local farmers' market.

olives, plain, or flavoured (page 40)
slices of Parma ham (prosciutto di Parma), or its Spanish cousin, Serrano ham
slices of delicious salami
pieces of roast pepper — good-quality bought, or homemade (page 133)
Chicken Liver Crostini (page 131)
Mushrooms with Herbs and Lemon (page 135)
Sun-Dried Tomatoes (page 134)
Salad of Aubergine and Olives with Rocket Leaves (page 136)

Roast Red and Yellow Peppers

Serves 8–10

2 red peppers, left whole
2 yellow peppers, left whole
olive oil

Preheat oven to 230°C/450°F/gas 8. Rub some olive oil over the peppers, then pop on a baking tray or glass plate and put into the hot oven. Cook for about 40 minutes or until very soft and a bit black. Take out of the oven, put into a bowl, cover with cling film and let cool. When cool, peel the skin off the peppers with your hands. Don't rinse in water, as you'll lose the flavour if you do. I find it helps to have a bowl of water nearby in which to rinse my hands. Using a butter knife, scrape the seeds out, which should leave just the flesh. Use as desired.

Sun-Dried Tomatoes

Sun-blushed tomatoes are basically not quite as dried as sun-dried; so, cook them according to your taste. They're great in pasta sauces, in a sandwich or salad, or on crostini. Very easy — all you have to do is cut small tomatoes (either very ripe, delicious regular tomatoes, or cherry tomatoes) in half, and place, cut side up, on a wire rack sitting on top of a baking or roasting tray. Season with salt, pepper and a pinch of sugar, and a small drizzle of olive oil, and balsamic vinegar (optional). Then, place in a very cool oven (I will assume you will cook these in the oven and not in the very hot sun), about 50°C/100°F/gas ¼ (if it is too hot, they will go dark and bitter). A fan oven works well for this too, and I would normally wedge the handle of a wooden spoon in the door of the oven to keep it ever so slightly ajar. Leave to 'cook' and dry out for about 18 hours; this sounds ridiculous, but keep in mind that if you are serious about this sun-dried tomato making, you could make kilos of the stuff at a time! Basically, when they look shrivelled up and almost dry, they're ready. If they cook for too long, they will be too strong in flavour, and if they don't dry enough, they won't be strong at all. They should keep for months, in a cool dark place (the fridge is good), in a sterilised jar, topped up with olive oil (you can use this oil later — it will be fab!) If they are not sufficiently dried, they will go off much sooner.

Mushrooms with Herbs and Lemon

Serves 4, or if part of antipasto plate, 10
Makes 1 x 300 ml (10½ fl oz) bowl

This is great to serve with a barbecue, too. It will keep for days.

3 tbsp olive oil
450 g (1 lb) mushrooms — buttons, flats, oyster mushrooms — sliced,
with the stalks discarded
salt and pepper
2 cloves of crushed or grated garlic
1 tbsp chopped marjoram, or ½ tbsp chopped thyme leaves, or parsley
1 tbsp lemon juice

Heat up a frying pan on a high heat. When hot, add the oil and sauté the mushrooms. Do not overfill the pan — sauté in batches if necessary. Toss on a high heat for a few minutes until golden and tender. Add the garlic, stir for a second on the heat, then remove from the heat. Add the herbs and lemon juice, and season to taste. Serve at room temperature.

Salad of Aubergine and Olives with Rocket Leaves

Serves about 8 as part of an antipasto plate

This is a gutsy salad that is great as part of the antipasto plate, or as a salad in itself (nice with some strong, salty Italian cheese like pecorino, or parmesan shaved over it). It's also delicious with fresh goat's cheese crumbled over it, or with some sun-dried tomatoes chopped and added too.

2 large, or 3 small, aubergines, thinly sliced
olive oil
50 g (2 oz) olives, stoned, and chopped
3 tbsp olive oil
sea salt and pepper
handful of rocket leaves

Brush the aubergine slices well with olive oil. Heat a frying or grill pan over a high heat and cook the thin slices of aubergine till golden. Transfer to serving plate. In a small bowl, mix the olives with the 3 tbsp olive oil. Add sea salt and freshly ground pepper to taste, and drizzle over the aubergines, while still warm. Scatter with rocket leaves when you are ready to serve. Serve at room temperature.

Watermelon Salad with Feta, Lime and Mint

Serves 4

This makes a great light meal in itself, served with Chilli and Garlic Pitta Crisps (page 130), or toasted tortilla chips on the side. It is a salad that I also love to serve with barbecued meats.

500 g (17½ oz) watermelon
200 g (7 oz) feta cheese, crumbled into pieces roughly 1–2 cm (½–¾ in)
square
finely grated zest and juice of one lime
1 tsp chopped mint

Peel, deseed and chop watermelon into 4 cm (1½ in) pieces. Place in a bowl, and add the crumbled feta, finely grated zest and juice of the lime, and the chopped mint. Toss gently and serve as soon as possible — best served within an hour or so of making.

NOTE Sometimes I add to this 50 g (2 oz) of toasted (in a moderate oven for 4 minutes or so) pumpkin seeds.

Ceviche

Serves 4–6 as a main course, or 10 as a starter

Ceviche, a speciality of many countries in Central and South America, is incredibly light and easy to digest. I love this kind of food — it makes you feel great. Do try to get the freshest fish possible.

750 g (1½ lb) skinned and filleted fish — sole, turbot, brill, cod or monkfish
pinch of sea salt and freshly ground black pepper
1 clove of crushed or grated garlic
juice of 4 limes, or 2 lemons and 1 lime
2 spring onions (about 25 g (1 oz)), finely sliced at an angle
½–1 red chilli, deseeded, and finely chopped
¼ large, or ½ small, cucumber, halved lengthways, seeds scooped out (and discarded) and cucumber chopped 1 cm (½ in) dice
2 tbsp coriander, or mint
1 large, or 2 small, avocados, finely diced 1 cm (½ in), or sliced
1 head of cos lettuce, or any other crisp lettuce
a few coriander leaves to decorate, or mint leaves if using mint

Slice the fish very finely, about ⅓ cm (⅛ in) thick. Place it in a dish, sprinkle it with salt and pepper, add the garlic and the lime or lemon juice, and leave it to marinate for two hours if possible (it does need at least 1 hour, for the fish to 'cook' in the citrus juice).

Then, add the spring onions, chilli, cucumber, coriander and avocado. Toss and taste for seasoning. Serve on a bed of lettuce leaves. Scatter with a few coriander leaves, and serve.

NOTE You can make this salad a few hours in advance if you have to, but don't put in the avocado until you are ready to serve.

Southeast Asian Pork Salad with Sweet Chilli Dressing

Serves 6 as a main course

This is another Southeast Asian-inspired recipe that gives you the wonderful sweet, sour, salty flavours. I adore a big plate of this for lunch or supper, summer or winter.

Don't be put off by the list of ingredients — many of the same items are used in both the marinade and the dressing.

450 g (1 lb) pork fillet (about 1 large pork fillet), trimmed of membrane, and sliced into 1 cm (½ in) slices

for the marinade:
2 stalks of lemongrass, outer leaves discarded, chopped finely
2 red chillies, deseeded and finely chopped
4 cloves of crushed or grated garlic
3 shallots, finely chopped
50 g (2 oz) dark brown, muscovado sugar
50 ml (2 fl oz) fish sauce
2 tbsp sesame or sunflower oil
50 g (2 oz) unsalted peanuts

for the dressing:
75 ml (3 fl oz) fish sauce
75 ml (3 fl oz) lime juice
2 red chillies, sliced into thin rounds
2 cloves of crushed or grated garlic
50 g (2 oz) caster sugar

for the salad:
½–1 head of cos lettuce, or any other crisp lettuce leaves, roughly torn
a large handful of a mixture of coriander and mint leaves
4 spring onions, finely sliced at an angle

1 cucumber, cut in half lengthways, deseeded, and sliced at an angle

Place the meat in a bowl. Add in the marinade ingredients, and stir. Place in a fridge and, if possible, marinate for 1 hour. While the meat is marinating, place the peanuts on a tray, and roast in a hot oven for about 5 minutes until golden, or toast on a frying pan on the heat. If there are skins on the nuts, rub them off at this stage, and discard the skins. Chop the nuts roughly.

Make the dressing for the salad by adding all the ingredients into a bowl or jar, and stir to dissolve the sugar; leave to sit. Prepare the salad ingredients by placing all in a lovely big shallow bowl, or plate, and keep in the fridge until ready to serve.

When you are ready to serve, place a grill pan, or frying pan on the heat. When the pan is hot and smoking, take the pieces of meat out of the marinade, and place in the pan. Cook for a minute on either side, then add the rest of the marinade ingredients and cook for another minute or two until slightly sticky. Take off the heat, and immediately toss the salad in the dressing, then add the pork in the sauce, and toss very quickly. Sprinkle the nuts on top, and serve straightaway.

NOTE The same weight of finely sliced beef sirloin or chicken breast works well in this recipe too.

A Big Bowl of Meringues, Bowl of Whipped Cream and a Big Bowl of Strawberries and Raspberries

This is such a lovely, simple way to serve pudding. It works perfectly if it is a casual get-together. Simply place a bowl full of mini pavlova meringues on the table, a bowl of softly whipped cream and a bowl of fruit — strawberries or raspberries or both — and, if you have one, a dredger with icing sugar or caster sugar. Get everyone to help themselves. It also means no work for you!

Use the Little Pavlova recipe on page 113, but make them even smaller if you like. A heaped teaspoon of raw meringue mix will give you cute little pavlovas and will take half the time to cook.

Raspberry Fool

Serves 4–6

200 g (7 oz) raspberries
juice of 1 lemon
50 g (2 oz) sugar
300 ml (10½ fl oz) cream — softly whipped

Whiz up the raspberries, lemon juice and sugar in a food processor, or simply mash with a fork or potato masher. Just before serving, gently fold into the whipped cream. Serve some Jane's Biscuits with the fool, if you like (page 38).

NOTE You can use frozen raspberries too, although fresh is better.

Chocolate

What would we do without some chocolate in our lives? Whether you are a die-hard fan of bitter-sweet dark chocolate, brown-sugary milk chocolate, or creamy vanilla-ey white chocolate, everyone seems to have their own favourite. As we now know, good dark chocolate, eaten in moderation, is actually good for us. So what more of an excuse do you need? For advice on melting, and choosing what type to buy, see page xiv.

Sweet and Sour Pork with Raisins, Pine Nuts and Chocolate

Serves 6

This recipe was inspired by a wonderful dish that we make at the cookery school, which originally came from Rome. The sweet–sour flavours and the gentle undertone of chocolate are truly delicious. In Italy, this gutsy dish would be served with a big bowl of creamy Polenta (page 144), but Plain Boiled Rice (page 190) works very well too.

2 tbsp olive oil
1.75 kg (3¾ lb) shoulder or leg of pork, cut into 3 cm (1¼ in) squares
(thick gigot chops, cut up, are fine)
2 onions (about 250 g (9 oz)), sliced
200 ml (7 fl oz) red wine
200 ml (7 fl oz) chicken stock, or water
salt and pepper
175 ml (6 fl oz) red wine vinegar
75 g (3 oz) sugar
50 g (2 oz) dark chocolate, chopped
150 g (5 oz) raisins
75g (3 oz) pine nuts, toasted on a dry pan, in a hot oven, for 2 or 3
minutes, till golden

Preheat an oven to 160°C/325°F/gas 3. Place a large saucepan, or casserole, on a high heat. When very hot, add the olive oil and brown the pork on all sides. Add the onion, and stir on the heat for a minute until the onion is slightly golden. Add the red wine and stock, and bring up to the boil. Season with salt and pepper, and place in the preheated oven. Cook for 1¼–2 hours (depending on the cut of meat), until it is lovely and tender. While the meat is cooking, place in a small saucepan the red wine vinegar and the sugar. Stir till the sugar dissolves, then boil for 2 minutes. Add the chopped chocolate, stirring to melt the chocolate, then add the raisins, and set aside to allow the raisins to plump up in the liquid. When the meat is cooked (it should be very tender; if it is not, cook it for longer), add the chocolate and vinegar mixture, and the toasted pine nuts.

NOTE If you want to make this a day in advance, it will only improve in flavour.

Polenta

Serves 6–8

This is what is sometimes called wet polenta, which is served in a big bowl, to accompany a hearty stew of some sort — as opposed to the dry or set polenta, which is cut into wedges and grilled.

1.75 l (3 pt) water
1½ tsp salt
225 g (8 oz) coarse or medium polenta flour (maize)
2 tbsp olive oil
50 g (2 oz) butter
50 g (2 oz) grated parmesan
freshly ground black pepper

Place the water in a large saucepan, and bring to the boil. Add the salt and the polenta, whisking all the time to prevent the polenta from going lumpy. Bring to the boil, then turn the heat down to very low. Stirring regularly, cook for about 30–40 minutes — until it's very thick. Stir in the olive oil, butter, and parmesan; and add some freshly ground black pepper, and salt if it needs it. Serve with the Pork with Raisins, Pine Nuts, and Chocolate (above).

Barbequed Lobsters and Prawns with Homemade Mayonnaise
(pages 180 & 5)

Butterfly Buns (page 209)

Dark Chocolate Ice Cream and White Chocolate Ice Cream (pages 155 & 156)

Kulfi (page 202)

Roast rack of Spring Lamb in a Guard of Honour, with Apple and Mint Chutney, Tzatziki, and Couscous with Lemon and Mint (pages 88, 90, 91 & 74)

Tom Yum with Chicken (page 185)

A Slab of Chocolate

Place a slab of your finest dark chocolate on a board in the centre of the table, with a knife for cutting it. Serve with small glasses of muscatel dessert wine or a sweet red dessert wine or port, or cups of espresso.

Berries with White Chocolate Sauce

Serves 4–6

This is the fastest pudding to make. Very pretty served in little bowls or glasses. The addition of orange zest and juice, or the liqueur, is optional.

400 g (14 oz) mixed berries — such as raspberries, strawberries, black-berries, blackcurrants, redcurrants. Fresh fruit is best for this.
100 g (3½ oz) white chocolate — chopped
2 tbsp water
½ tsp finely grated orange zest and 1 tbsp fresh orange juice OR 1 tbsp Cointreau/Grand Marnier (optional)

Place the berries in bowls. In a bowl suspended over a saucepan of simmering water, or in a microwave, gently melt the chocolate and water, stirring to combine. Add the orange flavouring if desired. Pour over the fruit to serve.

Chocolate and Almond Biscotti

Makes 20

Biscotti are the crunchy Italian biscuits, made for dunking into a glass of sweet Vin Santo, or a big cup of milky coffee, or indeed into a big bowl of hot chocolate! They will keep for a month or two, if airtight.

1 egg
100 g (3½ oz) caster sugar
125 g (4½ oz) plain flour
½ tsp baking powder
75 g (3 oz) roughly chopped dark chocolate
50 g (2 oz) whole almonds, skins on if you like, toasted for 8 minutes at 180°C/350°F/gas 4, until golden, and chopped
finely grated rind of 1 orange
1 dessertspoon milk and 1 tbsp sugar

Preheat an oven to 180°C/350°F/gas 4. Whisk the egg and sugar until pale and mousse-like, then fold in the rest of the ingredients (with the exception of the dessertspoon of milk and 1 tbsp sugar) and mix well. With floured hands, on a floured surface, shape the dough into a log shape about 4 x 28 cm (1½ x 11 in). Place on a parchment-lined baking tray. Brush the log with milk and sprinkle with a little sugar, then bake in the preheated oven for 20 minutes, until just set and pale golden. Remove from the oven. Remove from the oven and allow to cool for 5 minutes. Then, with a serrated/bread knife, cut the log into roughly 20 slices at an angle, about 1 cm (½ in) thick. Place these slices flat on the tray and place in the oven. Cook for 4–5 minutes on each side, until pale golden and dry. Cool on a wire rack.

NOTE Sometimes I replace the chocolate with chopped dates and add 1 tsp ground cinnamon too. Or chopped candied peel is also good.

See photo between page 112 and 113.

Chocolate and Banana Cake

Makes 1 loaf, about 12 slices

This is a really good teatime cake, and is perfect for a picnic. The banana sweetens it nicely and helps to keep it moist, so it stays really fresh for 2 or 3 days, and, of course, it freezes.

75 g (3 oz) chocolate
110 g (4 oz) soft butter
125 g (4½ oz) caster sugar
2 eggs
125 g (4½ oz) self-raising flour
1 level tsp baking powder
1 rounded tbsp cocoa
2 medium bananas, peeled and mashed (really ripe ones are great for this)

Preheat the oven to 180°C/350°F/gas 4. Line with parchment paper a 900 g (2 lb/measuring 13 x 23 cm (5 x 9 in)) loaf tin. Melt the chocolate in a low oven, microwave, or in a bowl set over a pan of barely simmering water. With a wooden spoon, cream the butter, add the sugar, and beat well; then add the eggs one by one, beating all the time. Add the sieved flour, baking powder and cocoa, followed by the melted chocolate and the mashed bananas. Stir to bring together. Pour into the prepared loaf tin and place in the preheated oven. Cook for 50–55 minutes, or until a skewer inserted into the middle comes out clean. Cool in the tin for about 5 minutes before removing.

Chocolate Fudge Mousse

Serves 4–6

150 g (5 oz) dark chocolate
3 eggs, separated
75 g (3 oz) butter, softened
25 g (1 oz) caster sugar

Melt chocolate (page xiv). Cool ever so slightly, and beat in the 3 egg yolks, then the softened butter. In a clean bowl, whisk the egg whites until they form stiff peaks; add the sugar and continue to whisk till glossy, shiny and stiff. Fold into the chocolate mixture gently. Place in little bowls or glasses, or one big bowl, and chill to set for about 1 hour.

Milk Chocolate Fudge Mousse

Replace the dark chocolate with the same amount of milk chocolate.

White Chocolate Fudge Mousse

Replace the dark chocolate with the same amount of white chocolate. Sometimes I add the finely grated rind of half an orange to this also.

Chocolate Roulade with Raspberries and Cream

Serves 8

This is a delicious, slightly rich, yet very light, chocolate roulade (the chi-chi name for a swiss roll!) It is perfect for a dinner party. The sponge can be made up a couple of days in advance, then filled and rolled on the morning of your party.

sunflower oil to grease tin

175 g (6 oz) dark chocolate, chopped
6 eggs, separated
175 g (6 oz) caster sugar

200 ml (7 fl oz) cream
1 tsp finely grated orange rind OR 2 tbsp Cointreau, or something similar
1 generous tbsp icing sugar

250 g (9 oz) raspberries

Preheat the oven to 180°C/350°F/gas 4. Line a swiss-roll tin (about 23 x 33 cm (9 x 13 in), or even a slightly bigger one if that's what you have) with tin foil, then brush the tin foil well with sunflower oil, or something similar. (Have the tin foil coming up the sides of the tin as well.) Melt the chocolate (page xiv), and put it aside. Place the egg yolks and sugar in a bowl, and, using an electric beater (or a food mixer), whisk until you have a light mousse, then whisk in the melted chocolate. With a clean whisk, beat up the egg whites until they are just stiff, then fold very gently into the chocolate mixture with a spatula or metal spoon, to avoid losing volume. Pour into the prepared tin and bake for 16–20 minutes, until it feels firm around the outside and still a tiny bit soft in the centre. Remove from the oven, and cool for 10 minutes. Cover with a damp tea towel, and keep somewhere cool for an hour, though it will keep for 2 days like this. While the roulade is chilling, whip the cream, add the orange rind and the icing sugar, and keep in the fridge. When you are ready to roll this — it is best rolled on the day that you want to eat it — remove the damp tea towel, place a sheet of greaseproof paper or tin foil on your work surface and dust with icing sugar (this stops it from sticking), turn the roulade onto this, and then peel off the oiled tin foil. Spread the flavoured cream over the roulade and sprinkle with raspberries; then, starting at the longest end closest to you, roll it up. Store it in the fridge until you need it, with the greaseproof or tin foil wrapping it and twisted at both ends like a Christmas cracker. To serve, transfer it to a plate. Don't worry if it has cracked a little — just dust it with lots of icing sugar, which will be very forgiving and look fabulous! Cut into slices to serve.

NOTE It is possible to freeze this — not at the rolled stage, but at the stage when it has been turned out onto the icing-sugar-dusted grease-proof or tin foil. Just cover it well in the freezer. To serve, thaw it first, then roll.

NOTE Feel free to add lots of different ingredients to the cream — such as 125 g (4½ oz) grated or finely chopped white chocolate; or sliced strawberries in place of the raspberries, or ½ tsp vanilla extract instead of the orange, or whiskey or rum, perhaps.

Double Chocolate Roulade

Make the roulade as above, but instead of the orange-flavoured cream, fill with Chocolate and Hazelnut Cream, as follows:

3 tbsp (100g (3½ oz)) of chocolate and hazelnut spread — e.g. Green and Black's, or Nutella
2 tbsp cream
300 ml (10½ fl oz) softly whipped cream

In a bowl, mix the chocolate spread with the 2 tbsp cream, then gently fold in the whipped cream. Chill until needed.

Easy Chocolate Sauce

Makes 300 ml (10½ fl oz)

125 g (4½ oz) good-quality dark chocolate, chopped into bits
200 ml (7 oz) cream

Bring the cream to the boil in a small saucepan. Take off the heat and add the chopped chocolate. Stir to melt the chocolate.

NOTE Sometimes I add other things into this, such as 1 tsp Cointreau, brandy or rum. For a very intense chocolate sauce, add 1 generous tsp of cocoa.

Chocolate Sorbet

Serves 6–8

This always brings me back to Italy. I love the intense chocolaty-ness of it, yet it is not creamy: divine. Again, you don't need a sorbet/ice-cream machine for this. If you like a slightly more bitter flavour, you could use a little unsweetened chocolate (see below).

225 g (8 oz) sugar
475 ml (16¾ fl oz) water
*250 g (9 oz) chopped dark chocolate (or 200 g (7 oz) dark and 50 g
(2 oz) unsweetened chocolate)*

Place the sugar and water in a saucepan, and stir on a medium heat until the sugar dissolves; then turn up the heat and boil the syrup for 4 minutes. Turn off the heat and immediately add the chopped chocolate. Whisk until the chocolate has completely melted in the syrup. Place in a bowl, and transfer to a freezer. Serve in little cups or glasses.

NOTE I used to take this out of the freezer a couple of times while it was freezing, and whisk it, to avoid getting a crystalline sorbet; but one time I forgot to, and it still turned out perfectly.

Chocolate Tart

Serves 12

This chocolate tart is smooth, creamy and divine.

1 x the quantity of Sweet Pastry (page 23), baked blind and cooled,
but still in the tin
150 g (5 oz) milk chocolate, chopped
150 g (5 oz) dark chocolate, chopped
200 ml (7 fl oz) cream
150 ml (5 fl oz) milk
2 eggs, beaten

Preheat an oven to 180°C/350°F/gas 4. Heat the cream and milk to almost boiling point, then take off the heat, and add the chocolate. Stir to melt all the chocolate. Let cool slightly for a few minutes, then stir in the beaten eggs. Pour the chocolate mixture into the baked pastry shell, and cook in the preheated oven for 17–20 minutes, until just softly set. Take out of the oven and cool for 20 minutes before taking it out of the tin (by placing the tart on top of a small bowl, the sides of the tin should be freed). If you want to take it off the base, wait for the tart to be completely cooled, but you can just serve it on the metal base on a plate, if you like. Dust with cocoa, or with icing sugar. This looks so pretty with some sugar-coated chocolate eggs on top — you can buy these in the pick-and-mix section of newsagents.

Chocolate Truffles

Makes about 40

These can be flavoured with a little alcohol if you like, just add 1–2 tbsp whiskey, brandy etc. to the melted chocolate cream, or the grated rind of half an orange. If you prefer, you can omit the stage of dipping into melted chocolate.

225 g (8 oz) dark chocolate, chopped
150 ml (5 fl oz) cream
cocoa powder

Place the chocolate and cream in a saucepan on a low heat, and stir until the chocolate has melted; continue stirring until the mixture is smooth. Pour out onto a shallow pie dish and allow to cool and set. Then, either roll into balls with wet hands (nice messy work!) or scoop with a melon baller or teaspoon (whlch you can keep dipping into hot water for easier scooping). Dip into melted chocolate (at room temperature, not warm) and then toss in cocoa powder. Serve with coffee after dinner.

NOTE Chopped roasted nuts are delicious too, added into the chocolate-cream mixture before it cools.

Dark Chocolate Ice Cream

Serves 8–10

This is a really good, rich, intense chocolate ice cream. It's quite quick to make, and you don't need an ice-cream machine to do it. It's great served on its own, or with a few fresh raspberries on the side; or for a serious chocolate fix, you could serve it with the white chocolate ice cream!

575 ml (1 pt) milk
150 ml (5 fl oz) cream
170 g (6 oz) dark chocolate, chopped
4 eggs
170 g (6 oz) caster sugar

Bring the milk and cream to the boil. Take off the heat, add in the chocolate, and stir until it has melted. In a bowl, whisk the eggs and sugar for about 5 minutes till pale and creamy. Add the chocolate cream to the egg mix, whisking all the time. Pour back into the saucepan, and place on a VERY low heat, stirring all the time for about 5 minutes, till the chocolate mixture is a bit thicker, like thick cream. It must not stick to the bottom of the saucepan, and it must not boil — if it does, it will scramble (push the mixture through a sieve if this does happen). Cool, then freeze overnight. Place the ice cream in the fridge for 5 minutes before attempting to scoop it. For a dinner party, it's a good idea to scoop it in advance (that morning, maybe) and place the balls of ice cream on a big plate on parchment paper in the freezer — then all you need to do that evening is lift them off the plate to serve.

NOTE To make a Mocha Ice Cream, stir in 2 tbsp (or more to taste) of Irel coffee essence, before putting in the freezer.

NOTE You can freeze this ice cream in a loaf tin lined with cling film, then cut into slices to serve.

NOTE If you want to put anything into this ice cream — such as chocolate chips, or broken Crunchie bar — stir it in when it is semi-frozen; otherwise the bits will sink to the bottom.

White Chocolate Ice Cream

Serves 8–10

This white chocolate ice cream is so rich and creamy, it's great served with the Dark Chocolate Ice Cream, or on its own, with some straw-berries, raspberries, or blueberries on the side.

575 ml (1 pt) milk
150 ml (5 fl oz) cream
225 g (8 oz) white chocolate, chopped
4 eggs
170 g (6 oz) caster sugar

Method as for Dark Chocolate Ice Cream (above).

See photo between page 144 and 145.

Divine Rich Chocolate Cake

This is the kind of chocolate cake that is perfect with a great cup of coffee or an espresso at the end of a meal. It's a great dinner-party dessert, is very easy to make and keeps really well for days and days and days.... As it's so rich, this size of cake would feed 8–10 people. If you prefer, you can dust the top of the cake with cocoa powder, or icing sugar, instead of the chocolate glaze. This also works very well using ground almonds instead of the flour — ground almonds give the cake a slightly more dense (in a nice way) texture.

1 dessertspoon melted butter, for greasing the tin
150 g (5 oz) dark chocolate, chopped
125 g (4½ oz) butter
150 g (5 oz) caster sugar
3 eggs, lightly beaten
55 g (2 oz) plain flour or ground almonds

for the chocolate glaze:
110 g (4 oz) dark chocolate, chopped
2 tbsp milk
45 g (1½ oz) butter

Preheat the oven to 160°C/325°F/gas 3. Butter the sides of a 20 cm (8 in) cake tin (or spring form) and line the bottom with greaseproof paper. Place the chocolate, butter and sugar in a bowl sitting over a saucepan of simmering water, and melt. Stir until smooth, then stir in the beaten eggs, and fold in the sieved flour. Pour the mixture into the cake tin and bake for 40–50 minutes until the centre is just set; allow to cool in the tin.

To make the chocolate glaze, melt all the ingredients together and stir until smooth. Allow to cool a little until it has thickened slightly (about 10 minutes) but do not place in the fridge as it will lose its sheen.

Take the cooled cake out of the tin, place on a plate or cake stand, and pour the glaze over the top, letting it drizzle down the sides too.

White Chocolate and Dried Cranberry Cookies

Makes 30–40

These are so yummy — and I feel that they are a tiny bit healthy too!
They keep perfectly for 4 or 5 days, and they freeze too.

150 g (5 oz) butter
150 g (5 oz) plain flour
½ tsp bread soda
50 g (2 oz) ground almonds
50 g (2 oz) porridge oats
50 g (2 oz) dried cranberries, or raisins, sultanas, currants
*50 g (2 oz) soft brown sugar and 50 g (2 oz) caster sugar OR 100g (4
oz) demerara sugar*
100 g (4 oz) white chocolate, cut into chunks
1 large egg yolk, or 2 small ones

Preheat the oven to 180°C/350°F/gas 4. Melt the butter, and allow to
cool. Sieve the flour and the bread soda into a bowl. Add the ground
almonds, oats, dried fruit, sugar, and the chocolate chips, and mix up.
Mix the cool melted butter with the egg yolk, and pour into the dry
ingredients, stirring to combine. With your hands, form into walnut-sized
balls and arrange slightly apart from each other on 2 baking trays.
Gently flatten the biscuits slightly, and place in the preheated oven for
8–10 minutes, or until golden. Allow to cool a little on the trays before
transferring them to a wire rack.

Irish Hot Chocolate

This is by no means a traditional Irish recipe, but it works very well for me in front of a good movie on a winter's night! Feel free to add something else instead of the whiskey — such as Cointreau, rum or brandy. Without the alcohol, children love it too.

Serves 2

200 ml (7 fl oz) milk
75 g (3 oz) milk chocolate
2 tsp cocoa
50 ml (2 fl oz) cream
2 tbsp whiskey

to serve:
2 tbsp whipped cream and 2 tsp grated chocolate

In a saucepan on a low heat, put the milk, chocolate, cocoa and cream. Stirring all the time, heat until the chocolate has melted, and the mixture has almost come to the boil. Take off the heat and add the whiskey. Add a tiny bit of sugar, if you like — though I find I don't need it. Pour into 2 cups, spoon the whipped cream on top, and sprinkle with some grated chocolate.

See photo between page 112 and 113.

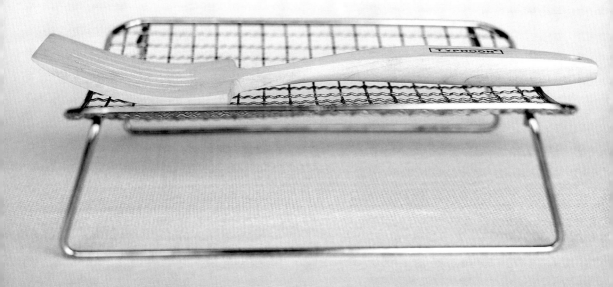

Barbecue

In our climate, we tend to think of barbecues only in the summertime, and even then the weather can be slightly unpredictable. But as with most barbecue food, in the event of a sudden monsoon-like shower, the food in this chapter can be cooked inside — either in an oven or, even better, on a grill pan (or started on a grill pan, and finished in the oven). There are also recipes here that don't actually get cooked on the barbecue, but are good to serve on the side.

Sea Breeze

Makes 4

This is such a good summertime cocktail — you can make up great big pitchers of these.

200 ml (7 fl oz) vodka
200 ml (7 fl oz) grapefruit juice (freshly squeezed is best, but not essential)
400 ml (14 fl oz) cranberry juice

Mix all the ingredients together, and serve over ice if desired.

Barbecue Salads

It's great to have a few salads to serve with all the barbecued meat and fish. These all work well:

- Potato Salad (page 162)
- Lemon and Basil Potato Salad (page 64)
- Spinach, Tomato and Feta Salad (page 163)
- Salad of Chickpeas with Red Onion, Tomato and Feta (page 164)
- Tomato and Avocado Salsa (page 46)
- Salad of Green Beans, Feta and Pine Nuts (page 66)
- Chunky Tomato Salsa (page 59)
- Greek Salad (page 62)

Potato Salad

Make a great big bowl of Potato Salad to have with a barbecue. Cook potatoes — if they are new potatoes, don't peel them; if they are not new potatoes, peel them after you have boiled them. Then cut into 3 cm (1¼ in) chunks — or into half if they are little new potatoes. While they are warm, drizzle the potatoes with just enough French Dressing (page 4) to coat them lightly, then allow them to cool while you prepare the other ingredients.

Make some Mayonnaise (page 5). Chop spring onions and lots of herbs, like parsley, chives, thyme, marjoram, tarragon, mint, etc. Then mix enough mayonnaise gently in with the potatoes to coat generously and fold through chopped spring onions and herbs. Season to taste.

NOTE Some crispy bacon would be nice too.

NOTE My brother-in-law, Dodo, makes a great potato salad; he adds chopped capers and gherkins.

Spinach, Tomato and Feta Salad

Serves 4 (or 6 as one of a few salads)

This salad is great with a barbecue, but also delicious to have with a simple pan-grilled lamb chop, or a beef steak! To prepare this in advance, add the spinach and tomatoes just before eating it.

4 tomatoes, quartered, or 12 cherry tomatoes, halved
200 g (7 oz) feta cheese
½ red chilli, deseeded and finely chopped, optional
¾ tbsp olive oil
1 tsp balsamic vinegar
salt and pepper
100 g (3½ oz) baby spinach

In a bowl, place the tomatoes and feta cheese. Make the dressing by mixing the chilli, olive oil and balsamic vinegar. Add salt and pepper. Add the spinach to the bowl and toss with enough dressing to coat the leaves. Serve immediately.

NOTE Sometimes I put in avocado in chunks.

Salad of Chickpeas with Red Onion, Tomato and Feta

Serves 4

This is a really good salad to have with a barbecue, or just great on its own with some feta cheese crumbled over it.

1 x 400 g (14 oz) tin of cooked chickpeas (drained weight 275g (10 oz))
50 g (2 oz), or one small, red onion, finely chopped
200 g (7 oz) cherry tomatoes, halved or quartered
1 tbsp chopped mint or parsley
1 tbsp olive oil
1 tbsp lemon juice
sea salt and pepper
100 g (3½ oz) feta cheese — crumbled into 2 cm (¾ in) chunks

Mix all the ingredients together in a bowl and serve.

This is lovely on its own, with feta cheese, in big chunks, mixed through it. It is also delicious for a simple lunch or supper with a pan-grilled chicken breast or lamb chop. I also love this as a filling for a warmed and split pitta bread.

Marinades for Barbecues

Isaac, my husband, always makes one or two marinades for the barbecue. Marinades not only give meat and fish fantastic flavour, but they also tenderise. If possible, give the meat or fish 8–10 hours to sit in the marinade, but 1–2 hours will be better than nothing. If you are having a very spontaneous barbecue, and have only about half an hour, it helps to score the meat slightly or even to bash it a little — this will help the marinade to penetrate the meat. (Don't do this with fish as it will break up if you do.) We use anything from lamb chops, pork chops and chicken breasts or legs, to sirloin or smaller minute beef steaks. Rub the marinade into the meat or fish very well, and rub it in more while it is sitting in the marinade, if you think of it. When you are ready to cook, just pull it out of the marinade (do not wipe it clean) and cook on the barbecue (or in a hot oven, or on a grill pan) until it is cooked to how you want it. I never add salt to the marinade as it will draw out the juice from the meat or fish, and dry it out. Season it with salt just before it goes on to cook. Give the meat 5 minutes to rest before serving, if you can.

These marinades make enough to flavour about 8–10 portions of meat or fish.

Yoghurt Marinade (for lamb, chicken, beef or fish)

300 ml (10½ fl oz) natural yoghurt
2 tbsp chopped mint or coriander
juice of 1 lemon
1 tbsp crushed cumin or coriander seeds
2 tbsp olive oil
2 cloves of finely grated or crushed garlic
a good pinch of pepper

Mix all ingredients together.

Saffron Marinade (for fish)

1 tsp saffron, soaked in 2 tbsp warm milk (or water)
1 clove of crushed or finely grated garlic
juice of 1 lemon
2 tbsp olive oil

Mix all ingredients together.

Ginger Marinade (for chicken, pork, beef, lamb or fish)

2 tbsp grated ginger
3 cloves of crushed or finely grated garlic
25 ml (¾ fl oz) olive oil
25 ml (¾ fl oz) Thai fish sauce
2 tbsp chopped coriander

Mix all ingredients together.

Herb Marinade (for chicken, pork, beef, lamb or fish)

100 ml (3½ fl oz) olive oil
juice of 1 lemon
a good pinch of freshly ground pepper
2 tbsp chopped marjoram (best for lamb and chicken), tarragon (beef and chicken), mint (lamb and chicken), coriander (all meat or fish) OR just 1 tbsp chopped sage (pork), rosemary (lamb and chicken), thyme (lamb, beef and fish)

Sometimes I add 3 cloves of crushed or grated garlic to this too. Or the grated zest of the lemon, for fish.

Spicy Peanut Sauce

Makes 250 ml

This could not be faster to make — slightly cheating with the peanut butter, but it works for me!

3 rounded tbsp peanut butter
½ deseeded chopped red chilli
2 cloves of crushed or grated garlic
2 tsp grated ginger
¼ tsp turmeric powder
1 rounded tbsp honey
2 tbsp soy sauce
1 tbsp lemon juice
4 tbsp (50 ml (1¾ fl oz)) water

Place all the ingredients in a blender or food processor and whiz until smooth.

NOTE This will keep perfectly in the fridge for 4–5 days.

Chicken Legs

Serves 4–6 (or more if one of a few things)

Adults and children love these – they have that wonderful Thai mixture of sweet, salty and chilli hot flavours! Not only are these great for a barbecue, but they're great cooked inside too, served with rice if you like.

1 kg (2¼ lb) drumsticks, or chicken pieces
2 red chillies, seeded and chopped
2 tbsp chopped coriander — leaves and stalks too
5 cloves of garlic, chopped roughly
2 tbsp brown sugar
juice of 2 limes (about 100 ml (3½ fl oz))
3 tbsp Thai fish sauce (Nam Pla)
1 tsp ground white pepper

Prick the skin of the chicken drumsticks with the prongs of a fork, about 3 times for each piece, and place in a dish. In a food processor, whiz up all the other ingredients, or if you are making by hand, chop up the dry ingredients, then add the remaining ingredients. Put the marinade over the chicken pieces, cover and refrigerate for a few hours or overnight if possible, tossing the chicken occasionally.

Bring the chicken to room temperature before cooking. If you are cooking these on a barbie, take the chicken out of the marinade (but leave on any little bits attached to the meat) and place on the barbecue to cook. They will take about 35 minutes. Start at a medium heat, and finish up for the last 10 minutes on the hottest part of the barbecue. Meanwhile, boil the marinade in a saucepan, uncovered for about 5 minutes, until it thickens slightly. Alternatively, place the chicken in a preheated oven at 230°C/450°F/ gas 8. Cook for about 35 minutes, until the meat comes away from the bone if you push it (same with cooking on a barbie). If the skin is not brown when it has finished, place under the grill for 5 minutes. Pour the marinade into a small saucepan and boil as above.

Serve the chicken with the sauce poured over or on the side.

Tandoori Chicken

Serves 4–6

I love this recipe. It's great cooked on the barbecue, or on a grill pan, or in a really hot oven (as hot as it will go), or of course the traditional way — in a tandoor oven. It really is best if it has 24 hours to marinate, but even 2 or 3 hours will be good. I love having some of the leftovers in a sandwich in pitta bread with Tomato Raita (page 187).

1 chicken, about 1.5–2.25 kg (3¼–5 lb), jointed and skinned (see Chicken Baked with Mushrooms and Marjoram, page 103), or about 6 large chicken breasts, or legs, or both!
75 g (3 oz) roughly chopped onion (about ½ an onion)
2 cloves of peeled garlic
1–2 red chillies, roughly sliced (I like to leave the seeds in for a bit of heat!)
2.5 cm (1 in) piece of ginger, chopped
1 tsp salt
250 ml (8¾ fl oz) natural yoghurt
3 tbsp lemon juice
2 tsp Garam Masala (I buy this in my local health-food shop, or see page 183)

to serve:
6 wedges of lime or lemon and Tomato Raita (page 187)

In a food processor, or liquidiser, whiz up the onion, garlic, chillies, ginger and the salt, then add the yoghurt, lemon juice and garam masala and whiz to a fine purée. Cut deep slits into the meat about 4 cm (1½ in) long — this will allow the marinade to penetrate further into the meat. Toss the chicken pieces into the marinade, rubbing it into the meat with your hands. Cover and place in the fridge to marinate, for at least 2 hours, better overnight.

When you are ready to cook it, remove the chicken pieces from the marinade, but don't wipe it all off, just whatever is clinging to the meat.

Place the chicken on a hot barbecue to cook on both sides until completely cooked — about 10–15 minutes on either side, depending on the heat of the barbecue. Or place the pieces on a roasting tray in a really hot oven for 25 minutes approx, or cook them on a hot grill pan, or even frying pan till cooked — all work well! Serve with a wedge of lime or lemon, boiled rice (page 190), Tomato Raita, and a very cold beer!

Beef with Lemongrass and Chilli

Serves 8

2 tsp chopped ginger
1 stalk lemongrass, chopped
½–1 red chilli, deseeded and chopped
1 clove of chopped garlic
1 tbsp toasted sesame oil
1 tbsp lime juice
2 tbsp Thai fish sauce (Nam Pla)
1 kg (2¼ lb) lean sirloin of beef, fat trimmed off and sliced about ½ cm (¼ in) thick
2 tbsp coriander leaves, scattered on at end

In a food processor, whiz up the ginger, lemongrass, chilli and garlic until you have a rough paste. Then add the sesame oil, lime juice and fish sauce. (If you don't have a food processor, just chop everything finely.) Place the beef in a dish and add the paste. Stir it around to make sure that all the beef is coated. Cover and chill for at least 1 hour if possible. This will improve the flavour and allow the meat to tenderise. Cook the slices of meat on a hot barbecue or on a hot grill pan for about 3 minutes on each side. Scatter the coriander leaves on top and serve with Spicy Peanut Sauce (page 168).

NOTE You probably won't need to add any salt to this as the fish sauce can be salty.

NOTE To prepare the lemongrass, remove and discard the tough outer leaves and the base of the stalk, and chop the rest. You can put the tough outer leaves into a teapot with the trimmings from the ginger and top up with boiling water to make a lovely nourishing tea — let it stand for 3 minutes first.

Barbecued Mackerel with Thai Dipping Sauce

Serve one mackerel, or half, per person

Metallic indigo-skinned mackerel are very plentiful in the summer. They are incredibly nutritious for us to eat — full of omega-packed goodness for the brain.

mackerel
olive oil
salt
Thai Dipping Sauce (page 174)

Slash the mackerel, just cutting through the skin a couple of times on each side. Drizzle with olive oil and rub it all over, then season with salt. Place on a hot barbecue or grill pan and cook on either side for about 5 minutes on a medium heat. Drizzle while warm with a little Thai Dipping Sauce and put some more in a bowl on the table.

Thai Dipping Sauce — to serve with the Barbecued Mackerel

Makes 250 ml (8¾ fl oz)

This dipping sauce transforms anything into an exciting frenzy of sweet, sour, salty and spicy flavours. Great with spring rolls, spicy lamb burgers, roast fish — you name it.

100 ml (3½ fl oz) Nam Pla, Thai fish sauce
100 ml (3½ fl oz) freshly squeezed lime or lemon juice (about 2 limes or 1 lemon, but measure to be sure)
75 g (3 oz) caster sugar
2 cloves of grated or crushed garlic
3 red or green chillies, sliced into fine rounds, with the seeds if you like it hot!

To deseed a whole chilli, if you don't like it very hot, cut off the stalk at the top. With the cut-side facing down, hold the chilli vertically between your hands and roll. The seeds should fall out the cut end.

To make the sauce, combine all the ingredients and stir to dissolve the sugar.

Butterflied Leg of Lamb
with Spices

We make this amazing recipe at the cookery school — this will feed 10 people easily, if they are having no other meat or fish. But with a selection of accompaniments, it would probably feed 25. You can, of course, halve the recipe. Leg or shoulder of pork works well for this too.

1 leg of lamb, about 3 kg (6¾ lb) in weight, butterflied

marinade:
2 tsp cumin seeds
1 tsp black peppercorns
1 tsp cardamom seeds
½ tsp chilli powder
1 tsp salt
5 tbsp olive oil
1 tbsp balsamic or white wine vinegar
3 garlic cloves, grated or crushed

Heat a pan. Add the cumin seeds, and cook for a few seconds, then add the peppercorns and cardamom seeds. Remove from the heat and crush coarsely. Mix with all the other marinade ingredients. Place the lamb in a large shallow dish or in a clear plastic bag. Pour the marinade over and rub into the meat. Leave for 24 hours if possible, rubbing the marinade into the meat every so often.

Drain the lamb from the marinade and place quite far (20 cm (8 in)) from the coals. It will take about 55–60 minutes to cook. Baste with the marinade a few times while it's cooking. Rest the meat for 10 minutes, then carve. You can also roast this, in all its marinade, in an oven preheated to 200°C/400°F/gas 6. It will take about 1–1½ hours. Baste it with the marinade regularly. Again, rest the meat before carving. Serve with Cucumber and Tomato Raita (page 187).

Chilli Barbecued Prawns

Serves 6 if giving everyone 3 prawns on a satay stick

These are so simple and easy and can be prepared early in the day.

18 tiger prawns, peeled and dried with kitchen paper
4 tbsp of shop-bought sweet chilli sauce
1 tbsp olive oil
6 satay sticks

Soak the satay sticks in water for 1 hour to prevent them from burning, or if you are stuck for time, boil them in water for 2 minutes. Take them out of the water and 'thread' each one with 3 prawns, or however many you like. The prawns should be parallel to the satay stick (the stick goes through each prawn twice). Mix the sweet chilli sauce and the olive oil. Place the prawns on a baking tray and spoon over the chilli sauce and oil. Turn the prawns over so that both sides of the prawns are covered in sauce. Leave to sit, if possible for an hour. Before placing on the barbecue or grill pan, wipe the exposed satay stick clean. Cook for about 5 minutes, until golden and cooked through. Scatter with coriander leaves.

NOTE For canapés, soak cocktail sticks in water, then thread just one prawn on each stick and cook on the barbie or a grill pan or under a grill.

Chargrilled Vegetables

Serves 4

Simple, easy vegetable kebabs always work well for a barbecue.
Change the vegetables according to your taste.

2 red onions, quartered, from top to bottom
1 small aubergine, cut into 3 cm (1¼ in) chunks
½ red pepper, cut into 3 cm (1¼ in) chunks
½ yellow pepper, cut into 3 cm (1¼ in) chunks
8 cloves of garlic, unpeeled
1 courgette, cut into 3 cm (1¼ in) chunks
3 tbsp olive oil
juice of ½ lemon
1 tbsp soy sauce
2 rosemary or thyme sprigs
4 metal or wooden skewers (or more smaller ones)

If using wooden skewers, soak them in water for 1 hour to prevent them
from burning on the barbecue. Place the vegetables onto the skewers —
a chunk of onion, aubergine, pepper, a clove of garlic, chunk of courgette,
and so on, till you have filled the skewers. Place in a gratin dish or roasting tray. Pour over the olive oil, lemon juice, soy sauce, and the sprigs of
rosemary or thyme. Turn in the marinade every so often, and leave for at
least 2 hours (if possible). If you really want to get ahead, you could leave
these overnight. I find that they are best if they are precooked in a hot
oven (220°C/425°F/gas 7) for 20 minutes in the gratin dish or roasting tray,
before cooking them on the hot barbecue for 10 minutes on each side.

NOTE Of course, you could add chunks of fish like monkfish, prawns,
or chicken, lamb or pork to this too.

NOTE Sometimes I add some stalks of asparagus to this marinade in
the gratin dish, and do not precook in the oven, but just pop them on
the barbecue for about 3 or 4 minutes on each side, then serve with
shavings of parmesan on top.

Little Fruit Kebabs

Soak cocktail sticks (or larger barbecue skewers) in water for 1 hour if they are wooden. Then thread onto them: strawberries (halved or quartered if they are large), chunks of banana, halved apricots, halved cherries, and chunks of nectarines or peaches. Place them in a gratin dish or pie dish, and sprinkle generously with muscovado sugar (and even a little Cointreau too, if you wish). Leave to sit for up to an hour, then place on the hot barbie, and cook for about 10 minutes, until just soft and a little scorched. Divine on their own, or with a little vanilla ice cream!

Barbecued Fruit Parcels

It's nice to have something sweet cooked on the barbie too. These can be made up earlier in the day — just cooked when you need them. In fact, they will only improve if prepared an hour or two in advance.

tin foil — cut/torn into rounds or squares, 20 cm (8 in) wide —
1 per person

a selection of fruit, like peaches, nectarines (cut into chunks, or 1 cm (½ in) thick slices) strawberries (halved if large), raspberries, blueberries, blackberries, bananas (cut into 2 cm (1 in) thick slices), mangoes (cut into chunks or 1 cm (½ in) thick slices), apricots (quartered).
sugar or honey — about 1 dessertspoon per portion
Cointreau, Grand Marnier, brandy, or rum — you get the picture! — OR
a squeeze of lemon/lime juice (about 1 tsp)
A tiny knob (1 cm (½ in) square) of butter per portion

to serve:
crème fraîche, or whipped cream, or vanilla ice cream

Onto the centre of each tin-foil sheet, place a handful of fruit (enough for 1 person), sprinkle with sugar or drizzle with honey. Add a splash of alcohol, if using (about 1–2 tbsp), or the lemon/lime juice. Finish off with a tiny knob of butter (of course you can leave this out, but it is rather good). Then bring the sides up to the top in the centre and 'scrunch' together to make a closed bag. Place in the fridge until needed.

to cook:
Place the parcels on the barbecue (I oil the bars on the barbie some-times — I don't want the tin foil to stick and tear), and cook for about 10 minutes, depending on the heat from the coals. Basically the fruit should be soft and very, very juicy, and hot — you can open one up to test. Give each person a tin-foil parcel on a plate, with warnings that they will be hot!

Other Things I Like to Cook
on the Barbecue

SWEET CORN — Drizzle the sweet corn, on the cob (you could cut the cobs in half if you like), with a little olive oil, and season with sea salt and freshly ground black pepper. Place sweet corn straight on the hot barbecue (or grill pan) and cook for about 10–15 minutes, turning regularly, allowing it to brown slightly. Take off the barbecue, and serve.

LOBSTER — Take your lobsters (they should still be alive!) and place them in salty lukewarm water in a saucepan (about 1 tbsp salt to every 1.5 l (2½ pt) water). Cover with a lid and bring up to the boil. Continue to boil for about 15–20 minutes, until the lobster has turned from navy blue to a deep orange colour. Pour off most of the water, leaving about 4 cm (1½ in) of water in the saucepan. Cover with a lid again and continue to cook for another 5 or 10 minutes, until they turn a quite bright orange. Take out of the water, place on a tray, and allow to cool. (This can be done earlier in the day.) Place the lobster on a chopping board with the hard shell of the back on the board, legs sticking up. Using a large chopping knife, cut the lobster in half lengthways — this takes a bit of muscle! Drizzle the cut surface with olive oil, and season with sea salt and black pepper. There's no need to remove anything — the brown meat in the head is sweet and juicy, and the white meat in the tail is firm and delicious. Place the lobster, cut-side down, on the hot barbecue (or grill pan) and cook for about 5 minutes, until the meat is browned — it will be so good! Take off the barbecue, and serve with Homemade Mayonnaise (page 5). I cook the lobster like this as the theory is that the lobsters think that they are in the lovely warm sea, then fall asleep as the water heats up, so they are all calm and the meat will be nice and tender — as opposed to sticking a knife in the back of their head to kill them, which people reckon toughens the meat! Anyway, I'm slightly squeamish at the best of times, so I'm afraid I couldn't do this!

PRAWNS — If I have lovely fresh 'Dublin Bay'-type prawns, I cook them first (heads and all, as they look so beautiful like this), like the lobster, just because sometimes they are still alive when we get them, and I cannot put a live prawn (or anything for that matter!) straight on the barbecue! So I feel slightly less cruel if I parboil them first! I would drop the fresh prawns in boiling salted water (same salt to water as the lobster), and bring the water back up to the boil quickly — this will take about half a minute. Then drain the prawns, dry them, drizzle them with a little olive oil, and place on the hot barbecue (or grill pan) and cook for about 2 or 3 minutes on each side, until nice and golden. To eat, separate the head from the tail, and peel the shell from the tail, dip into your mayonnaise (or flavour with herbs), and eat! Again, serve with a really good Homemade Mayonnaise (page 5). I often add some chopped basil, rocket or dill to the mayonnaise (about 1 or 2 tbsp) for the prawns or lobster. In my opinion, if I am going to the trouble of buying and cooking wonderful shellfish, it's worth serving an equally good mayonnaise!

See photo between page 144 and 145.

Curry Night

A curry is great when having friends over — you can make it (or nearly all of it) in advance, and it will only improve in flavour. It is also fun as you can serve as many different sauces and accompaniments as you please. For this reason, I wouldn't necessarily serve a starter first — just some spiced nuts with a cold beer — and more often than not, I would continue with beer to go with the curry. For dessert, I like to eat something cooling like the Indian ice cream, Kulfi, or Antony's Mango and Yoghurt Fool.

Garam Masala

Makes about 50 g (2 oz)

This is an Indian blend of spices — you can buy it ready mixed and ground in good ethnic stores, or health-food shops.

2 tbsp coriander seeds
2 tbsp cumin seeds
1½ tbsp black peppercorns
1 tbsp whole cloves
1½ tbsp cardamom seeds, taken out of green cardamom pods
¼ tsp freshly grated nutmeg

Heat a frying pan on the hob. Add all the spices except the nutmeg, and dry roast, stirring, until a little darker and fragrant — about 2 minutes. Add the nutmeg, remove from the heat, and allow to cool. Grind all the spices until fine (you probably need an electric spice grinder for this). Store in a tightly covered jar. This will keep perfectly well for about 1 month, and quite well after that.

Spiced Roasted Nuts

1½ tsp ground cumin
1½ tsp ground coriander seeds
½ tsp curry powder (use medium)
½ tsp ground paprika
½ tsp ground cayenne pepper
2 tsp oil
400 g (14 oz) shelled nuts, cashews, almonds, pistachios and peanuts
25 g (1 oz) fine caster sugar
1½ tsp salt

Preheat the oven to 150°C/300°F/gas 2. Measure all the spices into a bowl. Heat the oil in a frying pan, add the spices, and stir for about 30 seconds until lightly toasted. In a bowl, mix the nuts, sugar, salt and the toasted spices. Then spread on a baking tray or swiss-roll tin and roast for about 20–25 minutes in the oven — until golden and toasted.

NOTE If you want them with a bit more of a kick, add an extra ¼ tsp of cayenne pepper.

Poppadoms

Cook plain or spiced poppadoms in one of the following ways — either deep fried or under a hot grill. I usually like to cut the poppadoms into wedges before they are cooked. They take only a minute to cook, either way.

Tom Yum with Chicken

Serves 4

This is a wonderful, light, very 'clear' soup and can be made in minutes. Perfect for someone on a low-fat diet, it is also very satisfying and tasty.

4 stalks of coriander, leaves removed and roughly chopped, and stems put to one side
2 x 125 g (4½ oz) chicken breasts, cut into thin strips
3 x ¼ cm (⅛ in) thick slices of ginger (no need to peel)
1 green chilli, squashed with flat blade of a knife
¼–½ red chilli, deseeded and chopped
2 stalks of lemongrass, with outer tough stems discarded and squashed and bruised
1 l (1¾ pt) very light chicken stock or water
3 tbsp fish sauce
juice of 1 lime
5 basil leaves

In a saucepan, place the 4 coriander stems, the sliced chicken, ginger, green and red chilli and the lemongrass. Cover with a cold chicken stock (or water). Heat up and boil for 3 minutes, or until the chicken is cooked. Take off the heat and add the fish sauce, lime juice, the roughly chopped coriander and basil leaves. To serve, pull out the coriander stems, ginger, green chilli and lemongrass. In Thailand, these are normally left in, but for entertaining I take them out. You probably won't need salt because the fish sauce is salty enough.

If you have a cold or a hangover, this is the best thing.

See photo between page 144 and 145.

Tom Yum with Prawns

Serves 4

Instead of chicken, use 250 g (9 oz) tiger prawns, peeled and halved lengthways. If you don't want to use chicken or prawns, you could shred 1 head of bok choy and use instead.

Turkish Flatbreads

Makes 12

These are not breads traditionally made for curry, but I love to scoop up a spicy curry with them.

125 g (4½ oz) strong white flour
150 g (5 oz) plain white flour (you could use ½ white and ½ wholemeal flour here)
1–2 tsp of slightly crushed fennel seeds or cumin seeds
1 tsp salt
175 ml (6 fl oz) warm water

Mix the flour, spices and salt in a bowl. Add the warm water, and mix to a dough, kneading for 2 minutes. Divide into 12 pieces, cover and leave to rest — if possible, for 30 minutes. Roll out each piece of dough to ½ cm (¼ in) thickness, and cook on a hot dry frying or grill pan, on either side for about 2 minutes, until speckled with brown. Keep warm, wrapped up in a tea towel. They should be soft not crisp.

NOTE Sometimes I add 2 tbsp of chopped coriander into the dough, with the flour.

Tomato Raita

Serves 4–6

I love raitas. Sometimes I use tomato or cucumber, or both, or some-times banana. This also would be really good to serve in a pitta bread with left-over cold cooked Tandoori Chicken (page 170).

3–4 ripe red tomatoes, chopped into 1 cm (½ in) pieces
1 generous tbsp finely chopped onion, or spring onion, or red onion
1 clove of crushed or grated garlic
½ tsp ground cumin
½ tsp ground coriander seeds
225 ml (8 fl oz) natural yoghurt
salt and pepper, and a pinch of sugar

Mix all the ingredients together, and taste for seasoning. Don't prepare this too far in advance — any more than a couple of hours and it starts to go quite thin.

NOTE As always, I like to crush my spices freshly for this. I usually toast the spices on a dry frying pan for 1 minute or so — this gives a really good flavour, and it also makes the spices easier to crush, whether in an electric spice grinder, pestle and mortar, or, when cool, in a plastic bag and rolled with a rolling pin till crushed!

Cucumber and Tomato Raita

Makes 450 ml (¾ pt)

I love eating raitas with everything from curries, to barbecued meat, to left-over chicken in a pitta sandwich.

250 g (9 oz) tub of Greek yoghurt
½ cucumber, deseeded and finely diced
4 tomatoes or 16 cherry tomatoes, chopped
2 tbsp chopped coriander or mint
1 tsp ground cumin seeds
salt and pepper

Mix all the ingredients together. Season to taste.

Hot Chilli Sauce

Serves 6–8

For people who like their curry very hot, serve some of this on the side: beware!

4 red or green chillies, deseeded (though if you want this VERY hot, do not deseed)
125 g (4½ oz) onion (1 onion), cut into chunks
1 red pepper, deseeded and cut into chunks
3 cloves of garlic, peeled
pinch of salt and a pinch of sugar

Place all the ingredients in a food processor, and whiz. Store in the fridge for 2 or 3 days, or in the freezer. Add 1 tablespoon of water if it is dry.

Tamarind Chutney

Serves 6–8

Tamarind (which grows in Africa, India, Australia, and Southeast Asia) that we buy here is the compressed sour pulp extracted from the tamarind pod. The 'stones' or 'beans' in the pulp are too hard to eat so they need to be sieved from the pulp before making the chutney. This is really good with the Mild Madras Korma Curry (page 194).

50 g (2 oz) tamarind pulp
4 tbsp hot water
1–2 tbsp caster sugar
250 ml (8¾ fl oz) thick natural yoghurt (I use Greek yoghurt for this)
2 tbsp chopped mint or coriander

Place the tamarind in a bowl and add the hot water. Using your hands, mush up the tamarind, mixing it with the water to make a thick paste. Push this through a sieve — the tamarind stones will be left behind and can be discarded. Into the tamarind paste, add the sugar, yoghurt and the chopped mint or coriander. Add more sugar if it is too sour.

NOTE Sometimes I add 1–2 sliced bananas to this too.

Plain Boiled Rice

Serves 6-8

This is a very quick, easy and — dare I say it? — foolproof way of cooking rice. Sometimes I add some whole spices to the water and serve them on top of a bowl of rice — a small cinnamon stick and a few green cardamom pods, for example.

1 tsp salt
450 g (1 lb) basmati rice
15 g (½ oz) butter — optional

Fill a large saucepan with water and bring up to the boil. Add the salt and the rice, stir for a second or two and boil on a high heat for 4–5 minutes, or until the rice is nearly cooked (you should still have a tiny bit of bite — otherwise, the rice will stick later), then strain. Put the rice into a serving dish, stir in the butter, if using, cover with tin foil, a plate or a lid, and leave it in a low oven, 140°C/275°F/gas 1, for at least 15 minutes. It will sit for up to 30 minutes at 100°C/225°F/gas ¼. When ready to eat, remove the lid, fluff up the rice and serve.

Pilaff Rice

Serves 6

I absolutely love this method of cooking rice — it's practically foolproof, and ends up lovely and juicy and tasty.

25 g (1 oz) butter
1 small onion (about 125 g (4¼ oz)) chopped
300 g (10½ oz) basmati rice
750 ml (1¾ pt) chicken or vegetable stock
salt and pepper

In a saucepan that will fit all the rice, melt the butter, add the chopped onion, put on the lid and cook on a low heat until the onion is soft — about 10 minutes. Add the rice and stir on the heat for about 2 minutes. Add the stock and some salt and pepper. Bring to the boil then turn the heat right down to minimum and simmer on top of the stove, or in an oven at 150°C/300°F/gas 2, for about 10 minutes, until the rice is just cooked and all the liquid absorbed. Cover and keep warm if you need to.

Buttered Basmati Rice with Spices

Serves 6–8

A fantastic rice dish, full of flavour.

450 g (1 lb) basmati rice
800 ml (1½ pt) light chicken stock or water
1½ tbsp sunflower or vegetable oil
1 x 6 cm (2½ in) cinnamon stick
1 whole star anise
4 green cardamom pods, slightly crushed
4 cloves, whole
salt to taste
50 g (2 oz) butter, cut into small cubes

Put rice in a sieve and rinse in several changes of cold water, using your hands to mix the rice. Drain and place in a bowl and cover in fresh cold water. Soak for 30 minutes. Drain and rinse again. This will give the rice a wonderful, light texture. Into a large saucepan with a lid, place the stock, oil, cinnamon, star anise, cardamom, cloves and a good pinch of salt. Bring to the boil and pour in the rice, stirring. Bring to the boil again, then turn down the heat and simmer, without the lid and not stirring, until the liquid has almost been absorbed — about 7 minutes. Turn the heat down to very low, cover with a lid and let the rice steam for 10 minutes, until just cooked. Fluff the rice with a fork, add the butter, and serve.

NOTE This rice can be kept warm for about 20 or 30 minutes in a bowl covered with a plate.

Coconut Rice

Serves 6–8

450 g (1 lb) basmati or Thai fragrant rice
25 g (1 oz) butter
2 x 400 ml (14 fl oz) tins of coconut milk
1 tsp salt

Cover the rice with water, let it sit for 1 hour, then drain. Melt the butter in a casserole or heavy saucepan on a medium heat, add the rice, stir and cook for 2 or 3 minutes. Add the coconut milk and salt. Bring to the boil and cook gently without a lid, until all the coconut milk has been absorbed. Cover, turn the heat to very low and let the rice steam for another 10 minutes, until cooked. Serve.

NOTE This rice can be kept warm for about 20 or 30 minutes in a bowl covered with a plate.

Coriander Rice

Serves 4–6

This is basically plain boiled rice, but with added chopped coriander. This way of cooking rice is great — you can keep it warm really well for about half an hour, or of course you can reheat it. I normally reckon that 300 g (10½ oz) of rice (when raw) will feed 4–6 people well.

1 tsp salt
300 g (10½ oz) basmati rice
2 tbsp olive oil or 25g (1 oz) butter
2 tbsp chopped coriander (or mint)

Bring a big saucepan of water to the boil. Add 1 tsp salt and the rice, stir, and let boil for 5 minutes — by this stage, the grains should be three-quarters cooked. Strain through a sieve, and place the rice in a bowl. Stir in the olive oil or butter, and season to taste. Leave in a low oven, 140°C/275°F/gas 1, for 10–15 minutes, by which time it should be lovely and fluffy. If you want to prepare it half an hour in advance, put it into an oven at 110°C/225°F/gas ¼. To serve, mix in the chopped coriander.

Mild Madras Korma Curry

Serves 6

We have been making this recipe at the school for years now and I cannot find a better korma curry than this. It is mildly spiced but not hot. I would serve this with a hot chilli sauce on the side. Again, this will only improve if made a day in advance, and it freezes.

1 kg (2¼ lb) lamb (from the shoulder is good), cut into 3 cm (1¼ in) chunks

nut milk:

110 g (4 oz) nibbed almonds
450 ml (¾ pt) cream
1 tbsp grated ginger
pinch salt
25 g (1 oz) butter
4 onions, sliced
4 cloves of crushed or grated garlic
1 tsp cardamom seeds (from green cardamom pods)
2 tsp coriander
½ tsp black peppercorns
4 cloves
1 tbsp turmeric powder
1 tsp sugar
juice of ½–1 lime, or ¼–½ lemon

To make the nut milk, put the almonds into a saucepan with the cream and simmer for 4 minutes. Turn off the heat and allow the milk to sit for 15 minutes.

Mix the meat with the ginger and a good pinch of salt. Melt the butter in a large saucepan or casserole, and cook the onions and garlic for about 5 minutes. Grind the cardamom seeds, coriander seeds, pepper and cloves until fine. Add these spices to the onions and cook for 2–3 minutes. Turn up the heat and add the meat. Stir for a minute or two, then add the nut milk, turmeric and sugar. Stir and cover. Cook in a preheated oven at 160°C/325°F/gas 3 for about 60–70 minutes, or until the meat is tender. Add the lime or lemon juice to taste.

Serve with Plain Boiled Rice (page 190) or Buttered Basmati Rice with Spices (page 192), Hot Chilli Sauce (page 188), Tomato and Cucumber Raita (page 188) and some naan bread or Poppadoms (page 184).

Pork Vindaloo

Serves 6

My mother makes this fantastic hot curry. You can make a big pot of this for lots of people and, of course, it will only improve if made a day or two in advance. Vindaloos should be very hot, but use fewer chillies if you like. I've used lamb for this recipe too, with great success.

2 dried red chillies, or 3–4 fresh ones (with the seeds)
½ tsp ground turmeric
1 tsp whole black peppercorns
1 tsp cardamom seeds (taken from the green cardamom pods)
1 tsp black mustard seeds
2 tsp cumin seeds
a small stick of cinnamon — 2 cm (¾ in) long, or ½ tsp ground if you can't get whole
3 tsp ground coriander seeds
25 ml (1 fl oz) white wine vinegar
1½ tsp salt
1 tsp brown sugar
200 g (7 oz) onions (2 small onions) whizzed in a food processor till fine
sunflower oil
6 large cloves of garlic
2 tsp chopped ginger
1 kg (2¼ lb) pork shoulder meat, with no bone, cut into 2½ cm (1 in) cubes and no fat. Dried off on kitchen paper.

In a spice or coffee grinder, grind the chillies, turmeric, black peppercorns, cardamom, mustard, cumin, cinnamon and coriander. Place in a bowl and add the vinegar, salt and sugar. Set aside. In a wide pan (large enough to hold all the pork), fry the whizzed-up onions in 2 tbsp sunflower oil until golden, stirring regularly. Add the onion to the spices and vinegar — this is the vindaloo paste. Unless you burn the pan, you don't need to wash it.

In a food processor, whiz up the garlic and ginger (or grate them both finely), add 25 ml (1 fl oz) water and set aside. Heat 4 tbsp of oil in the same big pan over a high heat. In batches, brown the pork pieces, stirring regularly. Add more oil if necessary. Place the meat in a bowl and stir the garlic ginger paste on the heat for about 20 seconds, then add the pork and any juices back in. Add all the vindaloo paste and 250 ml (8¾ fl oz) water. Bring to the boil, cover and place in an oven preheated to 160°C/325°F/gas 3. Cook for 1–1½ hours until the pork is tender. Serve with a big bowl of Plain Boiled Rice (page 190).

Rajasthani Chicken Curry with Tomatoes and Yoghurt

Serves 4–6

This light, delicious curry will only improve if made in advance. Don't overly boil or the yoghurt will curdle, but it will still taste delicious.

1 chicken (cut into 6 or 8 portions; see page 103)
big pinch salt
4 tbsp sunflower oil
2 onions (about 250g (9 oz)) sliced
1 x 6 cm (2½ in) stick of cinnamon
1 tbsp grated ginger
4 cloves of grated or crushed garlic
1 tsp ground turmeric
1½ tsp paprika
¼ tsp ground nutmeg
½ tsp ground cumin
seeds from 4 green cardamom pods, crushed
½ tin chopped tomatoes (200 g (7 oz)) and a good pinch sugar
100 ml (3½ fl oz) water
125 ml (4½ fl oz) Greek yoghurt
coriander leaves to scatter on at the end

Dry the chicken pieces with kitchen paper and sprinkle with salt. Heat 2 tbsp of the oil in a large wide pan and brown the chicken pieces in batches till golden. Remove. Add a bit more oil if the pan needs it, place the onions in the pan and cook until soft — about 5 minutes. Add the cinnamon, ginger and garlic, and cook for another 2 minutes, then add the turmeric, paprika, nutmeg, cumin and crushed cardamom. Stir for a minute, then add the tomatoes, sugar and water, and cook for about 5 minutes. Add the chicken pieces, cover and cook on the hob (or in an oven preheated to 170°C/325°F/gas 3) for about 20 minutes, or until the chicken is cooked, then stir in the yoghurt. Remove from the heat, scatter with coriander leaves and serve with Buttered Basmati Rice (page 192).

Thai Red Prawn and Butternut Squash Curry

Serves 6

*1 x 400 ml (14 fl oz) tin of coconut milk, the thin milk separated from the
thick milk — they separate in the tin*
1–1½ tbsp red curry paste (watch out — it can overpower the whole thing!)
2 tbsp fish sauce
2 tbsp palm sugar or brown sugar
*450 g (1 lb) butternut squash, peeled, deseeded and cut into 1–2 cm
(½–¾ in) cubes*
*300 g (10½ oz) tiger prawns (300 g (10½ oz) with shells, 250g (9 oz)
without), peeled*
6 kaffir lime leaves — optional

Place the thick coconut milk in a wok or saucepan. Boil for about 6–8
minutes until it has thickened and it starts to separate. Add the curry
paste and fry for 4 or 5 minutes, stirring all the time. Add the fish sauce,
the sugar, the squash and the thin coconut milk and bring to the boil.
Boil for about 15 minutes until the squash is cooked. Add the prawns
and simmer for 2 minutes longer until they are just cooked. Add torn
lime leaves, if using, and serve.

NOTE You probably won't need salt as the fish sauce is salty enough.

NOTE Kaffir lime leaves are available fresh (you can freeze them) and
also dried (in many supermarkets), but if I don't have them, sometimes I
might throw in a few torn basil or coriander leaves instead.

NOTE You could also use other types of squashes or pumpkins for this.

Thai Red Curry with Potatoes, Squash and Broccoli

Serves 6

1 small head of broccoli
1 x 400 ml (14 fl oz) tin of coconut milk, the thin milk separated from the thick milk — they separate in the tin
1½ tbsp red curry paste
2 tbsp fish sauce
2 tbsp palm sugar or brown sugar
450 g (1 lb) butternut squash, peeled, deseeded and cut into 1–2 cm (½–¾ in) cubes
300 g (10½ oz) peeled and chopped (2 cm (¾ in) cubes) potatoes
6 kaffir lime leaves — optional

To prepare the broccoli, divide the florets into bite-sized pieces and put aside. Peel the thick stalks and chop into 1 cm (½ in) cubes. Bring to the boil about 500 ml (17½ fl oz) of water, with a good pinch of salt. Add all the broccoli (florets and stalks) and boil uncovered for 4 or 5 minutes, until just cooked. Drain and refresh with cold water. Set aside.

Follow the method for the Thai Red Prawn and Butternut Squash Curry (page 199), but omitting the prawns. Add the chopped potatoes at the same time as the butternut squash, and simmer until cooked. Add the cooked broccoli and simmer for one more minute. Toss in the kaffir lime leaves, or basil, or coriander and serve…

Sometimes I vary these vegetables — cauliflower works well with or instead of the broccoli.

Anthony Worrall Thompson's Mango and Yoghurt Fool

Serves 6–8

This recipe is from Anthony's great book, *The ABC of AWT*, and it is divine. It's just the kind of thing I like to eat after lots of spicy food, and I love the leftovers for breakfast too!

600 g (1¼ lb) (3 small tubs) Greek yoghurt
1 tbsp grated fresh ginger
1 tbsp ground cardamom (seeds from the green cardamom pods)
2 mangoes, peeled
150 ml (5 fl oz) cream
2 tbsp caster sugar
½ tsp vanilla extract

Combine the yoghurt with the ginger and ground coriander. Finely dice one of the mangoes and set it aside. Cut the flesh off the other and purée it in a food processor. For a very smooth purée, pass through a sieve. Mix the diced mango and purée into the yoghurt. Whip the cream with the sugar and vanilla extract, to soft peaks. Fold the cream into the mango yoghurt. Spoon the mixture into glasses or bowls and refrigerate until required.

Kulfi

Serves 6

This is an incredible rich, fragrant Indian ice cream. Fabulous to eat after a spicy curry, it's good with Poached Apricots with Cardamom too (page 114).

1.25 l (2¼ pt) milk
2 whole cardamom pods
seeds from 4 cardamom pods, crushed
75 g (3 oz) sugar
50 g (2 oz) chopped pistachios, plus extra for serving

In a heavy-bottomed pot, place the milk and 2 slightly bashed cardamom pods. Boil the milk down to 450 ml (¾ pt) — this will take about 1 hour, but I measure it to make sure. Turn off the heat, and remove and discard the cardamom pods. Add the sugar, nuts and ground cardamom seeds. Stir well. Leave to cool. Cover and freeze. Stir the kulfi every 20 to 30 minutes, to help break up the crystals. It will get harder to stir as it thickens. When it becomes too thick to stir, leave it to freeze solid. Keep covered. To serve, scoop some onto a plate or into a little glass bowl and scatter with chopped pistachios.

See photo between page 144 and 145.

Afternoon Tea

Proverbs, poems, books and films have all been written about or dedicated to tea. The American writer, Henry James (1843–1916), said 'There are few hours in life more agreeable than the hour dedicated to the ceremony known as Afternoon Tea.' Well, I think I must have been born in the wrong century. Whether it is to wake up in the morning, a mid-morning cup while the boys are at school, or an afternoon with friends and their children, I can always put some time aside to sit (most of the time!) and have a cup of tea, and what better excuse is there to have some cake too!

Almond Tartlets with Raspberry Jam and Cream

Makes 12 little tartlets

These are gorgeous little things, and so quick and easy to make. In Ballymaloe, we serve them for pudding, topped with fresh fruit, such as whole raspberries, but they work really well with a cup of tea with just the jam and cream.

50 g (2 oz) butter
50 g (2 oz) caster sugar
50 g (2 oz) ground almonds
about 50 ml (2 fl oz) raspberry jam and 75 ml (3 fl oz) whipped cream to finish
1 x mince-pie tray (shallow bun tin)

Preheat an oven to 180°C/350°F/gas 4. Cream the butter really well, until it is very soft. Add in the sugar and ground almonds, and stir to combine — do not beat it. Place teaspoonfuls of this mixture into the tin — no need to spread it out. Place in the preheated oven and cook for about 6–10 minutes (depending on your oven), or until a deep golden colour. Keep an eye on them as they burn easily! Let them sit in the tin for 2 minutes, before removing to a wire tray to cool. If they cool completely in the tin, they will stick. If that happens, just pop them back in the oven to 'unstick' themselves!

Arrange on a plate. Spread 1 tsp raspberry jam, then a little dollop of whipped cream on each, and serve.

NOTE The raw mixture for this can be made in advance. When they are cooked, the tartlets will keep well for a couple of days. Once they are decorated with jam and cream, they should be eaten within an hour or so.

Apricot Slice

Made as for Mincemeat and Almond Shortbread (page 25) but replacing the mincemeat with the mixture below.

300 g (10½ oz) dried apricots
juice of ½ orange

Whiz apricots in a food processor (or chop finely by hand). Mix with the orange juice and spread between the layers of shortbread, as with the mincemeat.

Raspberry Slice

These are good at any time of the year — with a cup of tea of course!

Make the same way as the Mincemeat and Almond Shortbread, but replace the mincemeat with about 200 g (8oz) (½ jar) of raspberry jam.

Madeira Cake

My mum nearly always has one of these made when I go home — either plain like this one, or with dried fruit or coconut, or with lemon rind, or coffee and nuts (see below!) These cakes are consumed with lots of cups of tea, and great chats! This recipe works well in a 900 g (2 lb) (13 x 23 cm (5 x 9 in)) loaf tin, or a 20 cm (8 in) round cake tin (with sides at least 5 cm (2 in) high), or an 18 cm (7 in) square tin, or a swiss-roll tin (see below). As you can see, the possibilities are endless!

a little butter to grease the tin
175 g (6 oz) soft butter (soft butter is the key to a good, light sponge, though it shouldn't be melted)
175 g (6 oz) sugar
3 eggs
1 tsp vanilla extract (optional)
225 g (8 oz) plain flour
1 tsp baking powder
2 tbsp milk

Preheat an oven to 170°C/325°F/gas 3. Butter around the sides of a round 20 cm (8 in), or square 18 cm (7 in) cake tin, and place a grease-proof paper disc, or square, on the base; or line the loaf tin with grease-proof paper. In a bowl, cream the butter. Add the sugar and beat for a minute. Add the eggs one by one, beating all the time, then the vanilla. Fold in the sieved flour and baking powder, followed by the milk. Scoop all this into the prepared tin, smooth the top, and place in the preheated oven for 55–65 minutes, or until a skewer inserted into the centre comes out clean.

NOTE I have 2 pieces of non-stick baking paper (available from super-markets and kitchen shops), cut and prepared for 2 loaf tins, so I can use these over and over again, and just wipe them clean every time — very handy.

NOTE Another delicious way to enjoy the Madeira cake is with 2 generous tbsp of warmed honey (just place a bowl of honey in some boiling water for 5 minutes) gently brushed over the cake at the end.

The variations of the Fruit Cake, Coconut Cake, Coffee Cake and Lemon Tea Cake work perfectly in either the loaf tin, or in the cake tins too.

Fruit Cake

As above, but add 75–100 g (3–3½ oz) dried fruit (e.g. sultanas, raisins, currants), 50 g (2 oz) chopped candied peel (optional), and 2 tsp mixed spice (optional) with the milk at the end.

Coconut Cake

As above, but add 75 g (3 oz) desiccated coconut in with the flour.

Coffee Cake

As above, but add 1 generous tbsp coffee essence (I use Irel. In the UK, it is Camp) in with the eggs. When the coffee cake is cooked and cooled, make an icing by creaming 50 g (2 oz) butter, and adding in 100 g (3½ oz) sieved icing sugar and 2 tsp coffee essence; mix to combine. Spread this carefully over the top of the cake. Scatter with 25g (1 oz) chopped toasted walnuts, pecans, hazelnuts, or almonds. Sometimes my mother adds the chopped nuts into the actual cake mixture — this is lovely too.

Lemon Tea Cake

This is delicious — another variation of the Madeira Cake. Just add the finely grated zest of 1 large or 2 small lemons to the butter at the start of the cake mixture. Then make the 'glaze' by mixing the juice of 2 lemons with 100 g (3½ oz) of caster sugar. When the cake comes out of the oven, prick all over the top with a skewer or a cocktail stick, and pour over the glaze while it is still warm. It will get nice and crunchy as it cools.

Lemon Squares

Made exactly as above, but spread the cake mixture evenly out into a buttered swiss-roll tin 33 x 23 cm (13¼ x 9 in), and cook at 180°C/350°F/gas 4 for 20 minutes, or until the skewer comes out clean. Pour over the glaze as above. Cut into squares. Store this, if you like, in the swiss-roll tin (as long as it is not aluminium). These will stay very fresh for days.

Coffee Squares

Made as above, but add 1 tbsp coffee essence in with the eggs. Make an icing by creaming 100 g (3½ oz) soft butter, and mixing in 200 g (7 oz) icing sugar and 3 tsp coffee essence; stir to combine. When the cake is cooked and completely cooled, gently spread the icing to cover the top. If you like, you can then sprinkle over 75 g (3 oz) of chopped toasted nuts, such as walnuts, pecans, hazelnuts or almonds.

Butterfly Buns

(also called Angel Cakes, or Fairy Cakes)

Makes 24 mini butterflies or 12 medium butterflies

This is basically a Madeira cake mixture, so you could make plain buns if you don't want to have butterflies with wings. Of course, you could also flavour these like you can do with the basic Madeira. I love these in their very pretty, old-fashioned way, and needless to say children adore them too!

110 g (4 oz) butter
110 g (4 oz) sugar
2 eggs
¼ tsp vanilla extract
140 g (5 oz) plain flour mixed with ¼ tsp baking powder

about 100 ml (3½ fl oz) raspberry or strawberry jam
about 200 ml (7 fl oz) chilled stiffly whipped cream OR plain butter icing (see below)
icing sugar, to dust

butter icing:
Cream 100 g (3½ oz) soft butter. Add 200 g (7 oz) sieved icing sugar, ¼ tsp vanilla extract and 1 tbsp milk. Mix to combine.

Preheat an oven to 190°C/375°F/gas 5. Using either 1 medium bun tray for 12, or a mini-bun tray that holds 24, fill with paper cases. Make as for the Madeira Cake (page 206), or if your butter is nice and soft, throw the butter, sugar, eggs, vanilla, flour and baking powder into the food processor and briefly whiz, just until the mixture comes together, then divide evenly into the bun cases, and place in the preheated oven. Cook for 8–12 minutes, or until golden; the centre of the buns should just feel firm. (The mini buns may take only 5 minutes.) Cool on a wire rack. Then cut a slice horizontally from the top of each bun and cut each slice in half. Spread ½ tsp or so of jam on the top of each bun, then spoon or pipe whipped cream or the butter icing on top of that. Arrange the two half slices vertically into the cream on top of each bun to resemble butterfly (or angel, or fairy!) wings. Dust with icing sugar.

See photo between page 144 and 145.

Ginger Biscuits

Makes about 50

This recipe makes a lot, but they do keep well for a 4 or 5 days easily, and of course you can freeze them. Add more ginger if you like them quite spicy.

225 g (8 oz) soft butter
225 g (8 oz) caster sugar
2 big tbsp golden syrup (150 g (5 oz))
1 egg
450 g (1 lb) flour
2 generous tsp ground ginger
1 level tsp bread soda, sieved

Preheat the oven to 180°C/350°F/gas 4. Whiz up all the ingredients together in a food processor until they come to a soft dough. Or, if you don't have a food processor, cream the butter, add the sugar and the golden syrup, followed by the egg, then stir in the flour, ginger and the bread soda.

With your hands, form into walnut-sized balls (about 20 g (¾ oz) in weight) and place them on a baking tray — no need to butter or flour this. Flatten them slightly. You will need 2 or 3 baking trays, or make them in 2 or 3 batches. Place in the preheated oven and cook for 10–15 minutes until they are a golden brown. Take the trays out of the oven and allow to cool a little before removing them to a wire rack.

Cinnamon and Orange Biscuits

Made as above, but replace the ginger with ground cinnamon, and add the finely grated rind of 1 large orange.

NOTE I sometimes replace the cinnamon and orange with the grated rind of 2 lemons.

Marmalade Gingerbread

Serves 8–10

This is a really, really delicious cake — lightly spiced, with the mild orange flavour from the marmalade — and it keeps really well too. Absolutely perfect with a cup of tea. My sister loves this for breakfast with a cup of coffee!

75 g (3 oz) butter
150 g (5 oz) golden syrup
225 g (8 oz) marmalade (½ a 450 g (1 lb) jar)
225 g (8 oz) self-raising flour
4 tsp ground ginger
2 tsp ground cinnamon
1 egg, beaten
2 tbsp milk

Preheat an oven to 170°C/325°F/gas 3. Butter the sides of a 20 cm (8 in) cake tin, and place a disc of greaseproof paper on the base. In a saucepan, melt the butter, golden syrup and marmalade on a medium heat, stirring to combine. Allow to cool slightly for a minute. Sieve the flour, ginger and cinnamon into a bowl. Add the beaten egg and the milk to the slightly cooled mixture, and pour this onto the dry ingredients, folding it in to combine. Pour the mixture into the prepared tin, and place in the preheated oven. Cook for 40–50 minutes, or until a skewer inserted into the centre comes out clean. Cool in the tin for 10 minutes, then remove to a rack.

Shortbread

Makes 8 slices

For this book, I really wanted to include a recipe for proper Scottish Shortbread, so I rang my sister–in–law, Penny — Scottish girl that she is. She then rang her mother, so this is Annette's version and I love it. Annette says that you can press this into a round cake tin (20 cm (8 in)) to cook, or you can have it just freestanding on the tray (it doesn't spread while cooking), and that's how I like it, with the pattern from the fork prongs around the edge. The important thing with shortbread is that the butter must be nice and soft. I buy rice flour (different from ground rice) in the health-food shop.

140 g (5 oz) plain flour
25 g (1 oz) rice flour or cornflour
50 g (2 oz) caster sugar
100 g (3½ oz) soft butter
1 tbsp sugar, for sprinkling

Preheat the oven to 140°C/275°F/gas 1. In a bowl, mix the flours. Add the sugar. Then, with your hands, mix in the butter until it comes together — it will if you really knead it. On a baking tray, or swiss-roll tin, form it, with your hands, into a round disc, measuring 18 or 20 cm (7 or 8 in) in diameter; it should be 1–1½ cm (½–¾ in) thick. Pat it on top to smooth it out, and use a fork to prick it all over. Then, if you like, score the edges all around with the fork. Place in the preheated oven, and cook for 50–60 minutes, or until firm and pale golden. Leave it on the tray for at least 10 minutes when it comes out of the oven, but before it cools, cut the round into 8 slices, sprinkle with sugar, and transfer to a wire rack to cool.

NOTE If you like, you can make little round shortbreads — just form into walnut-sized balls in your hand, and squash slightly with a fork. I find these take just 20–30 minutes to cook — again, until they are firm and pale golden.

Tea Brack

This is a really good, moist tea brack. It gets even better after a couple of days!

Makes 1 x 900 g (2 lb) loaf

200 ml (7 fl oz) strong tea (it can be left-over tea)
150 g (5 oz) muscovado or soft brown sugar
50 ml (2 fl oz) whiskey
300 g (10½ oz) dried fruit (e.g. sultanas, raisins, currants; sometimes I add chopped candied peel too)

1 egg
150 g (5 oz) plain flour
1 tsp baking powder
2 tsp mixed spice
1 tbsp honey — optional

While the tea is still warm (or heat it up if it has gone cold), stir in the sugar, then add the whiskey and the dried fruit. Allow to sit overnight.

Next day, preheat the oven to 170°C/325°F/gas 3, and line a 900 g (2 lb) loaf tin, 23 x 13 cm (9 x 5 in), with parchment, greaseproof or non-stick paper. Beat the egg and add it into the fruit and tea mixture, then fold in the sieved flour, baking powder and mixed spice. Pour it into the pre-pared tin and bake it for 60–70 minutes, or until a skewer inserted into the centre comes out clean. Brush with the honey, if desired, and allow to cool in the tin for at least 20 minutes before taking out. Serve in slices, with or without butter.

NOTE A couple of times, I have allowed the fruit to soak for 2 nights, as I have forgotten about it, and it does make an incredibly good moist brack. Also, if I want this in a hurry, and have not been soaking the fruit overnight, I have boiled the tea, sugar and dried fruit for 2 minutes, before adding the whiskey, and allowing to cool completely.

Index